BETTER SAFE THAN SUED

KEEPING YOUR STUDENTS AND MINISTRY ALIVE

ONE WAY DO NOT ENTER

JACK CRABTREE

ZONDERVAN®

ZONDERVAN.com/
AUTHORTRACKER
follow your favorite authors

youth
specialties

**youth
specialties**

Better Safe Than Sued: Keeping Your Students and Ministry Alive
Copyright 2009 by The Livingstone Corporation

Youth Specialties resources, 300 S. Pierce St., El Cajon, CA 92020 are published by Zondervan, 5300 Patterson Ave. SE, Grand Rapids, MI 49530.

Library of Congress Cataloging-in-Publication Data

Crabtree, Jack, 1949-
  Better safe than sued : keeping your students and ministry alive / by Jack Crabtree. — [Rev. ed.].
      p. cm.
  ISBN 978-0-310-28261-7 (pbk.)
  1. Church group work with youth. 2. Safety education. 3. Accidents—Prevention. 4. Liability (Law)—United States—Popular works. I. Title.
  BV4447.C73 2008
  259'.23—dc22
                                                                2008026365

Cover design by Toolbox Studios
Interior design by David Conn

Printed in the United States of America

08 09 10 11 12 13 14 • 20 19 18 17 16 15 14 13 12 11 10 9 8 7 6 5 4 3 2

**THIS BOOK IS DEDICATED TO
MARY LU MASTERSON**

Thank you for the unconditional love and support
you have shown to me and the Youth for Christ staff.

CONTENTS

INTRODUCTION

This book provides general guidance to youth group leaders about a variety of complex legal issues. It is not a substitute for legal advice. Laws vary from state to state. Readers are therefore urged to consult a local attorney regarding their particular questions, and before using any of the specimen legal forms included in this book or on the accompanying CD.

This book is loaded with real life lessons learned from 35 years in active youth ministry. As a youth leader you will eventually learn all these lessons—either by instruction or experience. My goal is that you would learn these youth ministry safety lessons now, by reading this book, rather than through the kinds of experiences that can lead to your students being seriously injured or killed or your ministry being discredited. It's my hope that the students and families you serve will grow in faith through the care you showed them while they were involved in your youth ministry.

ALL THE STORIES ARE TRUE!

Everything you read in the following pages really happened to me or one of the many other youth leaders I interviewed for this book. Some stories are clearly identified with a real name and place; I changed the names and nonessential circumstances of other stories to maintain the privacy (and sometimes, to avoid the embarrassment) of those who contributed to this book. When just a first name is given, the name is fictional and unrelated to the real name.

I'M A VIOLATOR!

I'm no safety nut. You won't catch me wearing protective goggles and carrying a clipboard with 99 safety checkpoints. When the pages that follow sound preachy, remember that I'm a fellow sinner in safety matters (other matters, too). I'm guilty of laziness, procrastination, fear, overconfidence, and all the other basic reasons we let safety slide. Preparing this material has reminded me repeatedly about how generous God has been in protecting the students under my leadership when I have been poorly prepared to guard their well-being. I have a few years' head start on most of you, but we all have a lot of room for improving the way we protect the health and safety of our young people.

AVOIDING LAWSUITS IS NOT THE PRIMARY GOAL!

Being sued is a big deal. It can cost enormous amounts of time and money. It destroys friendships, generates negative publicity, and creates negative perceptions toward good people and valuable organizations. I'd like to keep you out of the courtroom, but there is a more compelling motivation for safety in youth ministry. Your role in youth ministry is a significant opportunity to communicate God's love, truth, and life to young people and families. Make it your goal that every young person and parent involved in your ministry would say your words and actions showed how much you loved the kids.

THE CD INCLUDES MORE RESOURCES!

The CD that accompanies this book includes a wealth of additional information you can use to help make your ministry safer. You'll find sample forms that can be modified for your use, an evaluation tool that can help you consider safety concerns within your own ministry, and printable handouts for use when discussing safety issues with your ministry team or preparing for particular events. Use these resources to equip your ministry and its staff and volunteers to better care for kids.

THIS BOOK IS NOT COMPLETE!

No doubt you have learned or will learn safety lessons not included in these pages. In areas of first aid, insurance, liability, legal requirements, sexual abuse, and group activities, I did my best to touch the main points. But I encourage you to keep learning in each of these areas. Safety and liability in youth ministry are growing concerns in our society. Churches and religious youth organizations are being held to a new level of accountability.

I HAD PLENTY OF HELP!

My sincere thanks goes to many people who provided much needed assistance and encouragement to this project. Special thanks to:

- Dave Veerman and Bruce Barton of The Livingstone Corporation and Jim Galvin (formerly with Livingstone) who conceived this idea, gave me an opportunity to develop it, and patiently guided me through the process. The entire team at Livingstone gave me lots of help.

- All the youth workers and youth pastors who honestly told me their stories and shared their struggles with safety issues. I've kept my promise to keep their names out of print. This is the one book in which no one wants their name mentioned.

- Becky, my wonderful wife, for her patience and support during my writing projects and her marvelous, steadfast love to me.

Every year I am increasingly thankful to Mary Lu Masterson and her family. Our lives are welded together because of the tragic death of Mary Lu's daughter Kim in 1990 when she was under my care on a youth trip. You can read my account of that terrible day in chapter 17. Mary Lu and her family gave me and our other ministry leaders their love and support during the worst tragedy a mother and family can experience. I am thankful God has kept our lives connected during the 18 years since we lost Kim.

"Those who trust in themselves are fools, but those who walk in wisdom are kept safe" (Proverbs 28:26).

If you have a youth ministry safety story to tell or if this book has provoked any change in the way you do ministry, drop me a note. I still have plenty to learn.

Jack Crabtree
Long Island Youth for Christ
1775 New York Avenue
Huntington Station, NY 11746
www.liyfc.org
jcrabtree@liyfc.org

THIS SHOULDN'T HAVE HAPPENED

CHAPTER 1

The bad news had been delivered. It was a no win situation. Larry, a 28-year-old youth pastor, stood in the doorway, halfway between the church van full of teenagers and the desk in the canoe outfitter's shop. In all the planning for this trip, he had never even considered this problem.

He stared at the swollen river just 150 feet away, across the parking lot. How was he supposed to know this was the weekend the water was released into the river from the reservoir? What was he going to do—run the river or drive this van home?

The owner of the outfitter's shop had explained that only experienced canoeists had any business being on the river today. But Larry and the kids had driven three hours hauling a rack of six canoes for this special, one-day outing. The van was rocking side to side with the pent-up energy of teenagers psyched for a wild day running the river. Larry felt the pressure building.

Five minutes later Larry pulled the van and trailer into a parking lot a mile down the road from the outfitter's shop. He asked his crew of teenagers how many of them had canoeing experience. Only the hand of his volunteer leader went up to join his. With a look of resignation and a slight laugh, Larry shouted, "What are we waiting for?"

Within minutes of hitting the river, almost every canoe had capsized. Everyone was soaked and shivering in the frigid, fast-moving current. It was going to be an adventure.

LARRY: AWESOME YOUTH LEADER OR FOOL?

Several months later the youth group was still retelling the stories of how they ran the river. Most memorable and laughable was Patty being so wet and cold she turned blue and couldn't breathe. She was shivering so much she didn't have enough strength to get out of the water and back into the canoe. It wasn't until later that night at home that she was able to get warm.

A father overheard the conversations of the young people and approached Larry privately to express his concern. He asked Larry if he had recognized Patty's symptoms as clear signs of hypothermia, suggesting Patty could have lost her life that day in the river. He questioned the choice Larry had made to canoe given the condition of the river that day and the inexperience of the young people.

Larry deflected the parent's concern, assuring him no one had gotten hurt. More important was the fact the teens had a great time. Adventure and a few risks make the youth group exciting and more attractive to the non-churched teens they were inviting to attend. He said driving home would have hurt the positive image of the youth group. Larry added he was confident that God would protect them from any real danger. They have people in the church praying for the youth ministry. Driving them home without going into the river would have been a big mistake.

Larry continued his youth ministry, not giving another thought to the incident. Most of the students in the youth group still think Larry is an awesome leader. Fortunately, for Patty's sake, Larry didn't learn his safety lesson the hard way. Unfortunately Larry hasn't learned his safety lesson at all. He just keeps rolling along.

Don't think badly of Larry. He does care about his students and would never want to see any of them hurt. To him, discussion of safety concerns is boring and stifles the freedom and fun he promotes in the youth ministry activities. Safety warnings sound restricting and probably would squash the excitement and spontaneous fun the youth group is supposed to have.

Larry can't picture himself standing before his youth group reading off a list of precautions and regulations. Nothing would destroy the atmosphere of his group as fast as a safety lecture. It would make him sound like a parent. Fear and caution are signs of "thinking old." Larry prides himself in "thinking young."

Larry's attitude toward safety issues reflects the attitudes and practices of many youth ministry workers—both paid employees of the church or organization and volunteer leaders. Safety is one of the last concerns discussed as youth activities are planned and implemented.

WHAT IF PATTY HAD DIED?

Consider the consequences if Patty's adventure in that chilly river had ended differently. Suppose the hypothermia had advanced a few more degrees. Patty would have stopped breathing, and her heart would have stopped beating. How prepared was Larry to respond to this life-or-death crisis?

Imagine that the best efforts of the paramedics and hospital team were not enough to save Patty's life. How would it affect all the people involved?

- Grief, sorrow, and shock would ravage the youth group and the church.

- Heartbreak and deep sadness would hammer Patty's family, her boyfriend, and her best friends. They would cry out to God about why such a fine young woman had to die before reaching the most fulfilling years of her life.

- Eventually anger and blame would be leveled at Larry and the volunteer leader. The story of raising hands in the van would be public knowledge. People would be second-guessing Larry and condemning his decision to canoe the river.

- New, strong love-hate feelings would surface in the youth group. In one sense the tragedy would give them reason to comfort one another and deepen their connectedness. But the painful memories of Patty's death would make it hard to be together without that experience being foremost in their minds. It's likely many members would seek to escape this by reducing their involvement.

- Personal guilt would weigh heavily on Larry, the volunteer leader, and any student or adult who felt responsibility for what happened to Patty. Larry's personal effectiveness and work habits would likely suffer for an extended period. He would find it hard to concentrate for any length of time because his thoughts would keep returning to what happened that day on the river.

- Church leadership would conduct some kind of review concerning the accident. Larry's leadership and effectiveness would be closely reviewed. Parents would voice concerns about safety in all aspects of the youth program. Larry's status would be diminished in the eyes of many church leaders and parents.

- Most likely, Larry and the church would be sued in relation to Patty's death. The proceedings would continue for several years. The litigation would provoke rifts between all the people involved. The whole tragic story would have to be retold many times during the judicial process. Plenty of hard feelings would come between everyone involved around issues of responsibility, pain, negligence, and money. This day on the river, it would seem, would never go away.

- No one would come out of this chain of events untouched. Everyone would be changed. Relationships would change. Attitudes would change. Some individuals would grow stronger in their personal faith; others would feel their faith shaken and fall away from their commitment to Christ and the church.

- One constant would remain. Patty would be gone. What happened couldn't be undone.

For years Larry would examine and reexamine his motives for taking Patty and the group on the river that fateful morning. He would have to admit to himself that he'd never even considered the possibility of someone dying that day. When he made his decision, he was thinking about wasting a three-hour van ride and listening to the complaints of students who might question his "awesome" status as a leader if he'd talked safety and decided not to canoe.

Larry might imagine all kinds of creative alternative plans he could have used on that day if he'd said "No" to canoeing. Unfortunately, on the day of the accident, those thoughts never crossed his mind.

Of course Larry's attention to safety issues would change forever. He would have learned the safety lesson from the most severe teacher—the life-changing, tragic experience.

CHANGING ATTITUDES TOWARD SAFETY

In writing this book I interviewed more than 50 youth workers about safety issues in youth ministry. I asked each of them if there were specific situations that had provoked significant changes in their attitudes toward safety issues. Here's how they completed the sentence, "I never took safety seriously until…"

- "I got older and had children of my own."
- "I saw a student in my group get seriously hurt."
- "A friend in youth ministry was involved in a horrible lawsuit over an accident involving the youth group."
- "A parent asked me why I hadn't done something to stop the game in which a student was seriously hurt."
- "My church board of elders talked to me about our legal liability."
- "There was a close call where we escaped a serious injury, but I realized how careless we had been."
- "I got hurt myself during a weekend retreat."

FIVE MAJOR REASONS YOUTH WORKERS OVERLOOK SAFETY

I WAS YOUNG

Young leaders often feel indestructible. They believe nothing can hurt them. Challenges are to be accepted and overcome, not analyzed. The younger the youth worker, the less likely he or she is to be adequately concerned about safety. Young leaders don't have to give up their enthusiasm and energy, but when they face safety issues, they must force themselves to think like a person who has lived a few more years or surround themselves with the counsel of mature volunteer staff members with more real-life experience.

I HAD NO CHILDREN

Parents often seem overly cautious and careful to a youth worker—until that youth worker becomes a parent. Having a child sharpens a person's awareness of danger and safety. One important role of a parent is to think ahead and anticipate any potentially harmful situations. Parents *childproof* a room to keep children from encountering what could hurt them. The responsible youth leader thinks the same way as he or she prepares for the youth group meeting. It's a mindset more naturally embraced by parents who daily look after their own children.

I WANTED KIDS TO LIKE ME

No youth leader wants to spend every activity or trip saying "No" to the kids in the group. Not wanting to offend or drive away any young person, youth leaders are sometimes afraid to confront students involved in dangerous activities. The mature youth leader knows students are not offended if they are confronted in a personal, affirming encounter. Students don't want to be yelled at or condemned in front of their peers, but they do appreciate a respectful call to responsibility and maturity.

I COULDN'T AFFORD IT

Operating a safety-conscious youth ministry costs time and money. Most youth workers run their programs on a last-minute schedule, either because they are procrastinators or volunteers in a time squeeze. Many events and activities are planned with no thought given to the potential dangers present. Safety requires training leaders in specific subjects (such as first aid, water safety, and emergency procedures) that require a significant time commitment. How many youth leaders are willing to invest the time and money for such training?

I HAD NO EXPERIENCE

A few trips to the hospital emergency room with students injured during youth group activities will change a leader's attitude toward safety. Nothing beats firsthand knowledge. Unfortunately it is a painful and costly method of learning. Wisdom can also be gained by watching others and heeding the warnings and advice of those who have paid the price of actual experience. Pride and stubbornness, however, keep some people from learning by any other method than their own failures. It's a heavy price to pay.

> A few more excuses youth workers offer for resisting any serious safety emphasis in their programs:
>
> - "Nothing bad has happened to us yet."
> - "You can't think of rules for everything."
> - "If we follow all these safety rules, we won't be able to have any fun."
> - "Relax, God will take care of us."

REFLECT AND INTERACT

Stop and reflect on your experiences and decisions related to the safety of young people. Better yet, discuss these questions with your youth ministry team:

- What lessons have you learned about safety during your youth ministry?

- If you had been a volunteer leader with Larry that day at the river, what would you have said or done?

- What good or bad decisions have you made regarding safety or danger as a leader in youth activities?

- What decisions about safety have you made in your personal life? What influenced you to make those decisions?

- What has made you more aware of your safety responsibilities in youth ministry?

CARRYING PRECIOUS CARGO

CHAPTER 2

Bob had an eye-opening experience during his first year as a youth minister:

I was driving a vanload of students from my church to a youth conference in Washington, D.C. Just outside the city I noticed the brakes were almost totally gone. I pushed the brake pedal all the way to the floor with little response.

We were already late for registration so I decided to keep driving. I took it real slow and nursed the van the last 10 miles to the downtown convention center with practically no brakes. We arrived safely, and I felt like a hero for getting our group to the destination in time for the opening program.

A year later I wonder how I could have been so stupid. I had no idea what the roads or the traffic would be like that last 10 miles. I could have easily gotten the van into the situation where only a crash would have stopped us.

> **SUPPORT YOUR YOUTH LEADER**
>
> Youth leaders (like Bob) make better decisions when they know they have the support and resources from their churches or organizations to resolve any problems they encounter on a trip.
>
> A youth leader needs:
>
> - An emergency contact procedure where he/she can get assistance and advice from the home base.
>
> - A credit card or debit card for any repairs or special needs.
>
> - 24-hour Road Service policy for the van or bus being used.

I realize now my response to that crisis matched the way I handle personal car problems in my life. I don't have the patience or money to call a tow truck. I find a way to get my car home and fix it there myself.

The difference this time was that I was no longer responsible for just me. I had 13 kids with me who belonged to someone else. They were under my supervision, and I was responsible for their protection.

I now realize when I operate as youth minister, the decisions I make can no longer be what I am comfortable doing but must reflect what parents and my church leaders would want me to do.

THIS CHANGES EVERYTHING

As a youth ministry leader, you are no longer responsible for just your life. You are now responsible for the safety of every young person under your supervision and care. Your choices and decisions must reflect that expanded responsibility.

This is the key attitude transformation that every youth worker (like Bob) must experience to understand how the job has changed. In addition to the important job of communicating the Christian message to young people, a youth ministry leader must also provide a safe, responsible environment. Your role as youth ministry leader requires accountability to several important groups of people.

WHO IS COUNTING ON YOU?

As a youth ministry leader, you must be able to give satisfactory answers to the key questions asked by the people who put their trust in you.

THE PARENTS WANT TO KNOW:

- Are you protecting my child from danger and harm?

- Are you modeling a responsible lifestyle for my kid?

- Are you teaching my kid to make good decisions?

- Do you think about possible danger elements of activities before you ask my son or daughter to participate?

- Do you love my kid enough to say "No" when necessary?

THE SPONSORING CHURCH OR ORGANIZATION WANTS TO KNOW:

- Are you being a witness for Christ by showing care and concern for each person's safety?

- Will your actions bring sorrow to people under our care?

- Are you teaching and modeling maturity to our youth?

- Are you exposing us to any unwise liability?

- Will you bring us any bad publicity?

THE PARTICIPATING STUDENTS WANT TO KNOW:

- Are my friends and I safe with you?

- Will you pressure me to take chances I cannot handle?

- Are you concerned about my future?

- Am I going to have sad memories because of a careless accident?

THE INSURANCE CARRIER WANTS TO KNOW:

- Is our contract with your group a wise investment?

- Will you follow the rules and restrictions we specify?

- Will you do your job as our partner in protecting these young people?

Imagine you are Larry, the "awesome" youth leader from chapter one. If Patty had died that day in the river, how would you answer the questions from parents, students, and church members? Put yourself in Larry's place. Try to imagine the questions you'd be asked. Then let the answers come out of your mouth so you can hear how they'll sound to the ears of those who will ask the questions.

If you find difficulty forming the right words, make a promise to yourself to never let careless planning or thoughtless decisions put you in that position. Use all the information in this book to transform your youth ministry into an operation that is both fun and safe. Be committed to giving your students thrilling memories and a lifetime relationship with Jesus, while protecting their physical well being.

THE WORLD HAS CHANGED

Ensuring a safe environment when working with kids has never been easy. But we face some unique challenges as we minister to kids in the twenty-first century.

SOME PARENTS ARE OVERPROTECTIVE

Many parents today aggressively protect their children from a world they see as increasingly dangerous. They equip their sons and daughters with cell phones and expect them to report their where-abouts and any problems. These parents fear unknown people and situations that might potentially harm their children. They are very tuned in to their kids, especially if they sense any danger or threat to them.

SOME PARENTS ARE DISCONNECTED

There's another big block of parents who are less connected to their kids than ever before. These parents let teenagers raise themselves; these parents seem to insulate themselves from their teens and what is happening to them. Their kids make their own decisions while living like tenants in their parents' homes. These parents are uninvolved and difficult for a youth leader to engage.

MEDIA AND PUBLIC OPINION ARE QUICK TO REPORT INCIDENTS AND PLACE BLAME

Nothing is "accidental" any more. Every bad event has a cause and someone to blame for creating it or allowing it to happen. Media attention to any mishap involving young people is huge. Speculation, unconfirmed reports, and premature blame fill the 24-hour news cycles. The result is often undeserved bad publicity for a church or youth organization.

LAWSUITS ARE FIRST RESPONSE

North America is the most litigious society in the world. A lawsuit is the answer to any problem or accident. No church or youth ministry should operate without access to legal counsel and adequate insurance coverage.

CHURCHES AND NONPROFIT ORGANIZATIONS ARE NO LONGER PROTECTED

The days when church or community youth organizations were rarely sued are over. Recent news events regarding sexual abuse in churches and misconduct by youth leaders feeds growing negative public opinion regarding the trustworthiness of church-based youth organizations. Lawyers and public officials are bringing charges against church leaders suspected of wrongdoing.

THERE ARE NO MORE SECRETS

Nothing is private or hidden from sight these days. This could be a positive development. With phone cameras and surveillance cameras everywhere, you can expect to see video or text evidence of anything your youth ministry does (positive or negative) documented and posted on the Internet or sent electronically to people in your community. You can be famous or infamous in a very short period of time. When you do what is right, this heightened visibility can be a major positive for your youth ministry. When you don't, the odds of hiding the truth are low.

WAKE UP TO YOUR NEW YOUTH MINISTRY RESPONSIBILITIES

I JUST WANT TO HAVE FUN, NOT A LOT OF RULES AND PAPERWORK

Many youth workers falsely assume being safe means not having much fun. Deep in their minds they think if they decide to run a safe youth program, it probably won't be very enjoyable or effective in reaching kids today.

Safe programs can still be plenty of fun. Making the ministry both fun and safe and recruiting more qualified people does take extra planning and work, but the leader can be confident that all the fun won't come to an abrupt halt because of a serious injury that could have been prevented with proper planning.

Carelessness is sometimes just the result of laziness. Searching for fun activities, leaders grab the first good idea they find without giving it a thorough safety examination. A few minor changes or adjustments can turn a risky activity into a safe one without reducing the level of fun.

You can't stop all accidents. You can do the best possible job of planning and taking safety precautions and still see students get injured or even killed. There are many forces you cannot control. Your responsibility is to recognize the forces you *do* control and make them safe for the young people you love.

PLANNING AND PREPARATION PAY OFF WHEN ACCIDENTS HAPPEN

A large parachurch youth organization in the Midwest was preparing to take hundreds of students to Florida by bus for a special camp experience during Spring Break. Two months before the annual trip, the organizational leaders began a weekly training for the staff related to safety on that specific trip. When changes in policies and paperwork were announced, there was considerable grumbling by veteran staff members who had done this trip for many years without any major incidents or accidents.

On the last hour of their 24-hour return trip, one of their buses was sideswiped and overturned by a semi-tractor trailer.

Fortunately, no one was killed, but 15 kids were taken to five different area hospitals for treatment. The rescue workers reported they
had never seen a group of staff leaders so well prepared and able to
provide medical and contact information for the students requiring
care. The improved paperwork and extra training for such an event
saved invaluable time and got the students the help they needed.

When the organization held a follow-up meeting for parents
and students, the staff received an outpouring of appreciation from
parents who praised them for the outstanding professional care given
to their teenagers. The extra preparation and training paid off when
the unexpected happened.

REFLECT AND INTERACT

Stop and reflect on your experiences and decisions related to the
safety of young people. Better yet, discuss these questions with your
youth ministry team:

- When did you start to understand the responsibilities a youth leader carries for the safety and protection of the young people involved?

- In what ways is being a youth leader now different from when you were younger and involved as
a teenager?

- What parts of the safety and preparation requirements do you dislike doing?

CARELESSNESS KILLS

It's almost midnight on July 24, 1993. The parking lot is filled with police cars and ambulances. Their flashing lights bounce off the leafy trees guarding the entrance to the Cliff Cave Park near the Mississippi River. The news is grim. The dead bodies of four boys and two adult leaders from a youth organization have been recovered. The search continues because others may still be missing—no one at the scene has a list of everyone who came on the outing. This is a youth ministry nightmare come true.

According to a report in *Youth Today* (a monthly newspaper for youth workers), 16 boys and 4 adult counselors had entered the park in two white vans. Apparently, they ignored the "Road Closed" sign and drove around the barricade that had been in place for two weeks because the river had risen well above flood level. Many other youth groups had cancelled their outings to this popular park because of warnings about possible flash flooding—but not this group.

They had been taking groups of boys to the cave regularly that month. The staff member who organized the outing had been spelunking (cave exploring) on his own but had received no formal training or certification. He led the group in the cave based on the verbal instructions of a friend who had explored the cave previously but was not able to be with them today.

The group did not follow normal caving guidelines that advise dressing in long pants and having at least three light sources per person. They had only one flashlight for each team of three people.

When they were about 1000 feet into the cave, disaster struck. As they were crawling in a low passageway, the amount of water flowing in the cave began to increase. Within minutes the water was up to their necks, and the force of the current was sweeping them away.

Two adult leaders and 11 boys got out safely and called police. The search continued for hours looking for the lost boys and adult leaders.

In the aftermath of this tragedy, things only got worse. The parents of both the boys who died and those who survived sued the youth organization. The state department of social services put the organization on indefinite probation saying it "failed to provide the necessary support for the safety and well-being of the children."

WHAT WENT WRONG?

What mistakes did these youth workers make on this tragic day? Write your list below:

1. _____
   _____

2. _____
   _____

3. _____
   _____

4. _____
   _____

5. _____
   _____

More . . .

COULD THIS HAPPEN TO YOU?

You're probably saying, "No way am I going in a cave with kids after that story!" I don't blame you. It's easy to see the glaring mistakes after someone else makes them. We shake our heads and wonder how those leaders could be so stupid to ignore the danger and be so unprepared.

But when youth leaders get honest, you will hear many stories filled with bad choices and foolish actions. The only difference is that most of them haven't had the tragic results of this cave story. Many youth leaders have had potentially deadly close calls and have lived to tell about it (by God's mercy and grace).

These cave explorers weren't bad people. They were trying to help kids have a positive adventure and personal growth experience. They had enthusiasm and energy. They were right in there with the kids sharing the experience. There was only one problem—they didn't know what they were doing. They lacked wisdom and experience. They were careless and didn't take safety concerns seriously. Sadly they (and their boys) paid for it.

BECOMING A CAREFUL STUDENT OF SAFETY

You probably weren't selected to be youth ministry leader because you had a reputation for being safety conscious. You were selected because kids like you or because you know how to have a good time while communicating the gospel. But everyone connected with your youth ministry is quietly counting on you to run a safe program and take care of their kids.

It's all right to admit safety is not one of your major concerns or strengths as a leader. The fact that you are reading this shows your openness to starting from where you are and learning how you can grow as a youth leader who understands safety concerns.

Good youth leaders need to be students…

- of the Bible.

- of teenage development.

- of modern culture.

- of family relationships.

- of counseling.

- of crisis management.

- of safety.

Let's be honest—safety is a background concern. You don't get a lot of attention for running a safe ministry. It's like being an offensive lineman in football. No one notices anything you do until a defensive player gets by you and slams the quarterback into the ground. Then all eyes focus on you, and everyone asks why you didn't do your job. Learn this lesson now. Seldom will anyone discuss safety with you—until something goes wrong and someone gets hurt. Unfortunately learning your lesson *then* won't get a kid out of a wheelchair or bring someone back from the grave.

Safety is a huge assumption everyone makes about youth ministry. The people who hired you assume you will be safe and will not hurt any of the young people. The students and their parents assume nothing bad will happen to them and their friends. You assume God will protect you from harm. But safety is too important simply to be assumed. Safety should be an intentional priority that must be built into your youth ministry. How will you do it?

REQUIREMENTS FOR A STUDENT OF SAFETY

First, a youth leader needs to be committed to safety personally. You are the first line of protection. How will you be transformed into a safety-conscious person? Will you be motivated by the fear of liability or of what you'd tell a parent whose son or daughter was seriously injured or killed while under your supervision?

Fear is a powerful motivator—but it shouldn't be your primary reason for pursuing safety in your ministry. You should take safety measures primarily because you have a strong love for all the students involved. You don't want to see anyone get hurt.

Your commitment to safety means investing time to think ahead and plan a response to possible dangerous situations. This takes initiative. It's proactive, not reactive. It also requires an investment of money and people. The student of safety rejects the shortcut approach. Money spent to purchase quality equipment and hire skilled people to provide expertise for training and medical response is worth every penny, an invaluable investment.

Second, the student of safety is constantly improving his or her ability to assess risk and danger. That ability is gained only through experience. You can learn vicariously—by reading the true stories in this book and listening to others. You also learn through real-life experiences. Every time you lead a youth activity or trip, you pack away knowledge for future use. You hope and pray to learn all the important safety lessons without seeing any of your young people lose their health or their lives.

Developing this risk-assessment skill is like learning to drive a car. If you are smart you start cautiously, learning to control and stop the car. The foolish and reckless drivers hit the accelerator and think about how to stop safely only when it is too late and the damage is done. Erring on the side of caution is not a sin. Every activity and event you conduct broadens your safety and ministry experience and equips you for more demanding opportunities.

CAN YOU SPOT THE SAFETY RISKS?

It's Friday night. You're the adult leader of a church youth ministry. To give your students something positive to do on this weekend night, you decide to open the church gym and the youth room. No program. No planning. No problems. Right? Think again.

The lights are on. The basketballs are bouncing in the gym. The flat-screen television and Xboxes are playing in the youth room. Teens are scattered throughout the lighted section of the church. You opened the church at 7 p.m., and you'll lock the doors after everyone leaves at 10:00. Everything seems fine.

Stop and think. What potential risks or dangers await a youth leader who's just trying to help teenagers by opening the church to kids for a night of recreation and hanging out? Sure, you're not leading the youth into a cave, but are you assuming everything is "safe" just because the setting is familiar and comfortable for you? Open your eyes, and try to see the potential dangers in plain sight.

Here's a list of some potentially dangerous situations that might occur during this "harmless" night of youth activity at the church. Check the floor plan of the church (opposite page) and the appropriate numbers linked with the potential problems.

CHURCH MAP

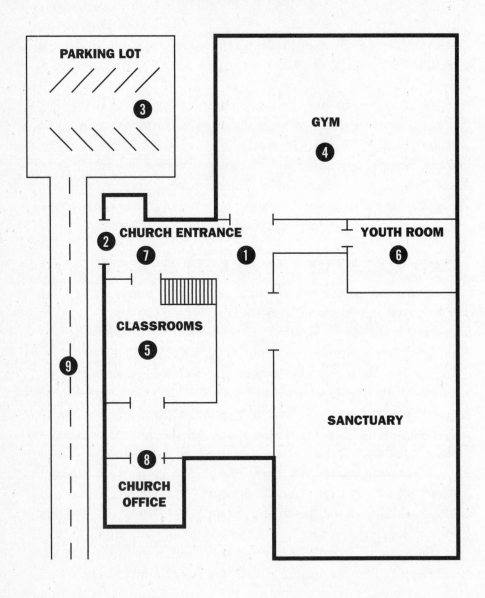

RISK 1: YOU ARE ALONE

None of the other volunteer leaders could make it tonight. Should that stop you? What would you do if a student needed emergency transportation to the hospital or home? With no other adult present, are you vulnerable to a false accusation of abuse by a student? Who would take charge if *you* were injured in the activities?

RISK 2: OPEN-DOOR POLICY

The kids in your group can walk in and out without asking your permission. You have no written record of who is present. There's a pizza parlor two blocks away where your students like to go for a quick snack. You've never had someone leave and not come back. Will tonight be any different?

RISK 3: EXCITEMENT IN THE PARKING LOT

Some of your kids have headed out into the parking lot to see another student's new car. You can hear the motor revving and the short squeal of the tires. They love to drive in circles with other kids sitting on the hood. Should you step outside and play the meanie?

RISK 4: ACTION IN THE GYM

The basketball game is only half court, but they are playing hard. You notice the mat that usually protects the wall under the backboard is missing. A couple of rectangular tables with metal edges (left over from the women's luncheon) are standing near one side of the court. At the other end of the court, some kids are trying to dunk the basketball by jumping off a metal folding chair as they run toward the basket. Each time they jump, the chair moves. They are falling on the floor and laughing hysterically. You know you'd hear plenty of groaning if you stopped all the action to fix these situations.

RISK 5: YOUNG LOVERS

You have two boy-girl couples that have been dating a while and are always hanging on to each other. Where are they now? Are they in the youth room watching DVDs or have they wandered down a dark hallway into another section of the church? Should you go looking for them?

RISK 6: LET'S GO TO THE DVD AND XBOX

The television screen is the only light in the youth room. It's hard to see who is bunched into all the couches. One of the students brought the DVD. You can hear gunfire and some bad language. Should you be monitoring what they watch on these nights?

RISK 7: THE EARLY EXIT

A cute 10th-grade girl tells you she's leaving now with some friends who will take her home. Should you let her go? And who are these "friends" waiting to drive away with her. You've never seen them before. When did they arrive? You know questioning her about this will make her feel uncomfortable in front of these friends. She assures you her parents won't mind.

RISK 8: WHO YOU GONNA CALL?

You have a cell phone. Is the battery charged after a long day at work? If someone were seriously hurt and you called 911, could you give the information needed to find you? If you had to take a student to the hospital, would the hospital be willing to treat that youth without a signed permission slip or parental release form for this activity?

RISK 9: THE DRIVE HOME

If you have to drive some kids home tonight, is your insurance coverage sufficient to cover the medical and liability costs for a carload of teenagers in case of an accident? What if the last kid you drop off (or the only one who needs a ride) is a young person of the opposite sex? If someone were to spread a rumor about your romantic involvement with a student, or if a student were to accuse you of a sexual advance, what recourse or protection would you have?

SHOULD WE ALWAYS BE AFRAID?

Does this list of risks make you permanently paranoid? The list of possible risks is endless. Is this a ridiculous list of fearful speculation, or is there an element of hidden (but real) risk every time you hold a youth ministry event?

Life comes with risk—we all live with risks and danger every day. Just driving a car reminds us how close we come to serious injury or death. A few inches or seconds either way could mean the difference between life and death. Nearly all of us have to admit that we've occasionally lapsed in our safe driving habits. Most of us have been fortunate that nothing serious happened. If we continue to ignore these little safety "wake up" calls, however, eventually we will pay for it.

The youth leader who overlooks the crucial role of safety in his or her ministry risks substantial losses in ministry opportunities, relationships, reputation, time, and money.

PRINCIPLES OF SAFETY

To create a safe youth ministry environment, youth pastors and volunteer leaders should teach and model these general safety principles. The remaining chapters of this book provide specific

> You'll find a printable copy of these safety principles on the CD with this book. Use it to help your ministry team discuss safety issues.

examples and instructions for common youth ministry experiences. If you and your team learn these principles, you will be prepared to face the new and varied youth ministry situations that will come in the future and apply them appropriately.

1. THE HIGHER THE RISK, THE GREATER THE SUPERVISION REQUIRED.

Meetings each week in the church youth room require a 1:15 adult leader-to-student ratio. But a weekend hike in the wilderness probably requires a 1:4 ratio. Raking leaves at the home of a senior citizen may require a 1:10 ratio, while handing out bag lunches on an international missions trip may call for a 1:2 ratio.

2. WHAT IS DANGEROUS? READ THE LIST!

Have you read you church or organization's liability insurance policy? Most policies include a list of excluded activities not covered by your insurance company. This list gives you a general guideline for what the insurance underwriters consider dangerous. Do your research. Most liability policies have a list of excluded activities and a list of activities with requirements (for example, wearing a helmet). Those exclusions are made on the basis of previous accidents.

Obviously activities that involve motorized vehicles, slippery surfaces, heavy physical contact, turbulent water, and hitting people with any type of projectile deserve special attention before you decide to proceed with your plans.

THE COMMON SAFETY SINS OF YOUTH MINISTRY

Which of these safety sins are present in your youth ministry?

- Not enough staff
- Too many kids in the vehicle
- No time to plan for safety
- No plan of action to respond to any emergency
- No use of seat belts
- No first aid training or supplies
- Inadequate paperwork (proper permission/medical forms)
- Letting a dangerous activity continue (afraid to stop it)
- Lack of background checks for volunteer staff
- Inappropriate conduct and sexual contact by staff with students

3. KNOW THE DIFFERENCE BETWEEN PERCEIVED DANGER AND ACTUAL DANGER.

There's often a big difference between perception and reality when it comes to what's dangerous. You can keep an atmosphere of fun and excitement in your youth program if you sponsor activities that look and feel dangerous but are, in fact, quite safe. A ropes course (in which students walk a single wire 20 feet off the ground) is both terrifying and thrilling to most young people. In reality a well-maintained-and-run ropes course is one of the safest experiences a young person can have because of the ever-present safety lines and high quality supervision. On the other hand most adults and students feel relaxed and complacent about safety around water when, in reality, the danger is much higher than they suspect (85 percent of all fatal accidents in the wilderness involve water).

4. PLAN FOR THE WORST-CASE SCENARIO.

The best training and preparation for an actual experience is discussing potential problem situations beforehand. Example: As you train counselors and drivers for the winter retreat, ask what they would do if their van (with 10 students) were separated from the rest of the caravan and developed engine problems. If they were 10 miles from the nearest town on a night when the temperature is five degrees above zero, how would they handle the situation? Help them talk through all their options and prepare them to make decisions when the real life events occur.

5. LEARN TO RECOGNIZE THE INITIAL SIGNS OF DANGER.

Great athletes have the ability to anticipate the opponent's next move. This enables the quick response that allows them to gain the victory. The safety-smart youth leader anticipates danger. If students are chicken fighting (one student riding on another's shoulders) in the small swimming pool, can you see the spot where the student riding on top might strike his or her head when he or she falls? Do you notice the signs that two young men are growing angry at each other during a competitive game and may begin using excessive force during the next round? Recognizing the initial signs of danger gives the youth leader the advantage to intervene before the accident happens.

6. KEEP IN MIND THE SPECIAL NEEDS OF YOUR GROUP.

Learn to make safety decisions according to the particular needs of the kids in your group. If a student has a severe peanut allergy, you may need to restrict the snacks eaten in the church van and talk to the camp director about not serving peanut products to your group.

7. TEST IT FIRST.

Bring your great idea—game, skit, or crazy activity—to life with a simulated trial run, using your staff as "crash test dummies." As you play you will be able to identify the danger points and make changes before you present it to the youth group.

8. RESIST THE SHORTCUTS.

Recognize the forces that will pressure you to shortcut your safety plans. When you are running late, you're more likely to skip the important step of checking the fluids in the van or giving your drivers printed instructions and directions. People will forget permission slips, first aid kits, and so forth. Don't let their "problem" pressure you to break important safety rules.

9. MAKE THE MOST OF YOUR MISTAKES.

Learn from your mistakes and the mistakes of others. Minor accidents or near misses are sometimes funny. But don't just laugh about them. Debrief with other leaders and talk about what could be done to make it safer next time.

10. TAKE THE "MY KID" TEST.

Treat each young person as though he or she were your own child. Don't put any student in a situation in which you would not place your son or daughter.

11. LEAD BY EXAMPLE.

The leader sets the pace for the volunteers in the issues of safety and every other matter in youth ministry. Don't bend the rules for your personal comfort or convenience.

12. BALANCE YOUR THEOLOGY.

Pray for God's protection, but exercise the thoughtful responsibility God has

---

BOOM! SUDDENLY EVERYTHING CHANGES!

Alan had the greatest job. Here he was in his mid-20s playing basketball in a small church gym with a group of guys from his YFC/Campus Life club. Spending time building relationships with these guys was what his boss wanted him to do.

He broke loose from his man and bolted toward the basket. On the way he tripped on the foot of another player, lost his balance, stumbled and crashed into the unpadded wall underneath the backboard. He laid on the floor motionless while the teenage guys stared at him in shock.

Today, Alan is living a productive life as pastor of an inner-city Presbyterian church, but when he moves, it's in a wheelchair. He has been paralyzed since that fateful day of basketball.

When you come to a gym to play basketball or a similar game and see no padded protective mats on the walls, what decision do you make?

given to you. Don't count on God to suspend the forces of nature and the laws of physics to protect you from the results of careless planning.

REFLECT AND INTERACT

Stop and reflect on your experiences and decisions related to the safety of young people. Better yet, discuss these questions with your youth ministry team:

- What close calls with injury or death have you had in your own life or in youth ministry?

- What did you learn from your own close call or from reading about the cave tragedy that will affect how you plan events for youth?

- How do you determine if you are being appropriately cautious or overly cautious with a potential youth activity?

- What principle of safety needs more attention in your youth ministry planning?

HOW SAFE IS YOUR YOUTH MINISTRY?

CHAPTER 4

It's time to assess the present level of safety in your youth ministry. Take a few minutes to evaluate yourself and your youth ministry team. Don't answer according to how you think it should be, but rather how it really is right now. This is a starting point for the leaders of a youth ministry to protect themselves, their church or youth organization, and the safety of the students and families they serve. You'll find a printable copy of this evaluation on the CD with this book.

Answer the following questions to focus on the vital safety issues in your youth ministry.

STAFF AND VOLUNTEER WORKERS
(Check One)

Yes	Sometimes	No	
☐	☐	☐	Have all staff and volunteer leaders gone through an application and acceptance process (including a written application, reference forms, background check, and interview)?
☐	☐	☐	Have all staff and volunteer leaders been screened for any criminal, sexual, or physical abuse accusations or violations in their past?
☐	☐	☐	Have all adult leaders been trained for the jobs they are asked to do?
☐	☐	☐	Have all leaders been trained in general safety procedures, as well as in specific safety procedures related to a particular activity or event?

☐ ☐ ☐ Are all staff and adult volunteers aware of and do they practice our ministry's standard of "safe conduct" with students to avoid any suspicion of sexual misconduct?

☐ ☐ ☐ Do all staff and volunteers know their jobs at the events they attend?

☐ ☐ ☐ Do we have an appropriate adult-student ratio at the events?

STUDENT INFORMATION
(Check One)

Yes	Sometimes	No

☐ ☐ ☐ Do we have a permission/release form and medical form signed by parent(s) and notarized for each participating student?

☐ ☐ ☐ Do we have current phone numbers to get in touch with parents in case of an emergency?

☐ ☐ ☐ Are parents fully informed (in writing) about the activities in which their children will be involved?

☐ ☐ ☐ If any of these students need to be taken to the hospital, are we prepared to answer the questions we will be asked about their personal information, medical information, and insurance?

FIRST AID AND EMERGENCY RESPONSE
(Check One)

Yes	Sometimes	No	
☐	☐	☐	Are the members of our youth ministry staff team trained in a certified first aid course?
☐	☐	☐	Is someone trained in first aid present at all of our youth activities and trips?
☐	☐	☐	Is our first aid kit adequately stocked and available at all of our youth activities and trips?
☐	☐	☐	Do staff and volunteers carry the phone numbers of important people who should be contacted in case of an emergency (ambulance, police, ministry supervisor, parents, etc.)

DRIVERS AND VEHICLES
(Check One)

Yes	Sometimes	No	
☐	☐	☐	Do we have a written policy on driving standards and who is allowed to drive for all the activities and trips?
☐	☐	☐	Do we only use drivers who are qualified and responsible?
☐	☐	☐	Do we prohibit students from driving other students to our activities?
☐	☐	☐	Do we require the use of seatbelts?
☐	☐	☐	Do we regularly check the vehicles we use for safety (fluids, brakes, tires, etc.)?

PLANNING AND PREPAREDNESS

(Check One)

<u>Yes</u>   <u>Sometimes</u>   <u>No</u>

☐   ☐   ☐   Do we have a clear written set of basic safety rules for the activities of the youth ministry?

☐   ☐   ☐   Do we have sufficient insurance coverage for both the leaders and students in the youth ministry?

☐   ☐   ☐   In preparing for an event, do we inspect the physical facilities or location and look for any safety hazards?

☐   ☐   ☐   In preparing for an event, do we walk through the proposed activities to anticipate the potential risks?

☐   ☐   ☐   Do we think through worst-case scenarios to identify potential problems and plan responses?

☐   ☐   ☐   Do we take the time necessary to ensure the safety of students who participate in our activities?

☐   ☐   ☐   When an activity appears to be dangerous, do we have the wisdom and courage to stop it regardless of the reaction of the students involved?

REFLECT AND INTERACT

Analysis: Each "no" or "sometimes" answer needs your attention. Review these questions and answers with your supervisors and your volunteer staff. Decide together what you can do to improve the protection you provide for the students in your youth ministry.

Where Do You Start? You cannot change all your safety standards immediately. Start with a few of the most important areas and work with your team to make them better. Continue to address issues and make improvements regularly.

SEXUAL MISCONDUCT

CHAPTER 5

As a youth leader the worst thing you can do is have some kind of sexual relationship with any of the kids in your care. Sexual abuse destroys lives, and it destroys ministries. An adult leader's sexual abuse of a young person is a devastating betrayal of the trust of everyone involved—including the student or students who are abused, their families, the other kids in your youth program, and the wider church or organization.

Sexual abuse is the number one concern of insurance providers when it comes to youth ministry. The past decade has seen a sordid history of sexual abuse of young people by church leaders. According to three of the biggest insurance companies covering churches, an average of 260 reports each year are filed, documenting sexual abuse of young people by clergy, church staff, volunteers, and church members in American Protestant churches. Since 1950 there have been 13,000 credible accusations of sexual abuse against Roman Catholic clerics—or 228 a year.

Counselors suggest the problem is far more prevalent than these numbers would suggest. It's estimated that less than 50 percent of sex abuse cases are reported. The number of young people who have been sexually abused and emotionally scarred by church people they once trusted may be higher than we'd ever imagine.

THE MAJOR SAFETY ISSUE OF OUR TIME

Sexual abuse of young people by church leaders is a legal issue and the primary reason for a growing number of lawsuits against clergy and counselors. Since the Roman Catholic sex abuse crisis became public in 2002, the church has been charged with covering up the truth, protecting the abusers, and ignoring the victims. Record financial settlements have been paid with more to come.

My greatest sadness and anger in 35 years of youth ministry is seeing co-workers, friends, professional ministers, and volunteers violate the sacred trust relationship by drawing teenagers into romantic and sexual relationships. Some of these crimes seemed almost predictable (because of a youth leader's reckless behavior); others have blindsided and shocked me—committed by people I never would have suspected. I've learned from experience how skillful a sex offender can be when he or she is hiding the truth.

THE TWO TYPES OF SEX OFFENDERS

It's important to understand that there are two different kinds of sexual offenders. **Preferential Sex Offenders** have a particular sexual interest in children. They actively seek children who match their preference and can have hundreds of victims. They pose a serious threat to churches because they often appear to be effective in working with kids. Many of the high profile cases in the Roman Catholic Church involved priests who had a long history of abuse with numerous children. Other preferential offenders have been coaches, teachers, and other highly regarded members of the community.

On the other hand, **Situational Sex Offenders** abuse children when the opportunity arises. They act on impulse. Many sex abuse cases connected to youth ministry fit in this category. The sex offender didn't have a plan to do this. It just happened because the offender was hungry for sex or affection or power and used his or her position of authority and trust to take advantage of a young person.

BEWARE OF SEX OFFENDERS

- One male, married youth leader had a real tight bond with all his junior high boys. He planned so many great special activities for the guys that the people of the church honored him repeatedly. He was very protective of his group and took a strong stand against cooperative events with other youth groups for theological reasons. Later the church learned the shocking truth. This model youth leader had numerous sexual encounters and relationships with the boys in his junior high group. An investigation revealed he had abused boys undetected in a previous church.

- A talented male, married youth leader started a home Bible study for his high-school girls in the home of one 16-year-old. Within a few weeks interest in the group Bible study waned, but he continued meeting alone with the girl. The Bible studies included back-rub massages, which led to him fondling her regularly. He knew it was wrong and a betrayal of his commitment to his wife, but he couldn't stop. Neither could he tell any of his friends in the ministry or his senior pastor. Eventually, the girl told her mother, who immediately went to the senior pastor. When the youth leader was dismissed, the rumor mill worked overtime.

- The police entered the church drop-in center. They arrested the male director in front of the volunteers and students and took him to jail in handcuffs. A 17-year-old girl had told her school counselor she'd been sexually involved with the director for over four years. During interrogation the male director admitted his sexual involvement and abuse to the police. It had started when the girl was 13, with few friends and newly divorced parents. He took advantage of her vulnerable situation and made her feel wanted and loved. The director kept this relationship a secret and successfully deceived his pastor and co-workers. After his arrest the drop-in center was closed. The kids who attended regularly were shocked and angry. The supporters and community leaders felt betrayed and embarrassed.

- A dynamic male youth leader developed a bad habit of focusing on several key students (usually girls) when they were on ministry trips. He would lavish these special girls with extra attention and win their loyalty with long, deep discussions about the hurts of life. Teenage girls loved to sit next to him and lean their heads on his shoulder while he talked about God's love. He knew one particular girl was especially open to him because of the recent disappointments in her life. She was eager for a major change in her life, hoping his faith would rub off on her. Late one night, after a long one-on-one talk, he attempted to take the relationship to a deeper level by kissing her on the lips. When she rejected his advances, he explained away the whole incident as a big misunderstanding. When the young woman told a counselor six months later, it set off an investigation uncovering this youth leader's history of similar abuse with other young girls who were vulnerable and trusting.

The level of sexual contact and criminality in all these cases is quite different, but the betrayal of trust is the common factor. Each of these ministry leaders crossed the line of moral and ethical behavior that parents expect when they put their children under the supervision and influence of a youth ministry. These adults willfully used their positions of influence to gain some emotional or physical satisfaction from one or more of the young men or women entrusted to their care. Each of them exposed the vulnerability of the youth in their care, took advantage of it for selfish reasons, and broke the trust.

WHEN STAFF BETRAY THE TRUST
THE KIDS ARE THE VICTIMS

Physically, young people who have been sexually abused may be forced to deal with pregnancy, abortion, and sexually transmitted diseases. Emotionally, they will be scarred by the seduction and betrayal. They are eventually dropped from "special status" with the adult leader. They feel the ridicule of their peers. Sometimes they are blamed for the dismissal of a popular youth leader. They feel guilt and shame for what they've done and the lies they've been forced to live. Their family relationships become increasingly tense. Spiritually, they may lose faith in God and in Christian leaders. They see hypocrisy everywhere and resist trusting any spiritual counselor. Guilt, shame, and depression may block their ability to pray. They often launch out in self-destructive behaviors, believing nothing in life really matters. It's crash and burn for them.

LAWSUITS AND/OR CRIMINAL PROSECUTION WILL FOLLOW

> **CHILD ABUSE**
> Child abuse is an abuse or misuse of power and authority over a child under the age of 18 by any adult who is responsible for that child.

In the past when young people were sexually abused by pastors and leaders in the church, it seldom led to a lawsuit or criminal action. These abuse survivors carried their secrets and their shame, convinced no one would believe their accusations against church leaders. They lived in a time when families were less prone to sue or expose such private matters to the public eye. Today, many of the taboos about legal action have been removed. Parents are still reluctant to put their teenagers through a public proceeding that would attract media attention; however, the number of young adults coming forward with allegations of being molested or abused while underage has increased dramatically. Adult leaders who get sexually involved with children or teenagers can expect to be looking over their shoulders for many years waiting for the anger to be released in some type of legal or criminal action. Churches and youth organizations can also expect to be charged with some type of negligence for allowing an employee or volunteer worker to harm a child.

THE BAD NEWS SPREADS

Parents, the media, the community, and students hear the news and judge the ministry accordingly. Consider how the public opinion of the Roman Catholic Church has been damaged by revelations about sexual abuse, even though the crime involved just a small percentage of the clergy. Everyone believes the worst about the priests who remain and serve faithfully. Bad news travels like wildfire, even when it isn't true. The sins of one person can bring down the good reputation of an entire church or youth organization.

THE YOUTH MINISTRY ATMOSPHERE CHANGES

Staff and students feel betrayed by the offender and the church as a whole. The exposure of the leader's hypocrisy leads people to be much more skeptical about all leaders, their faith, and their involvement in the youth ministry. Relationships are strained as people wonder what other secrets in the group have been hidden. Students and adults experience shock and go through the steps of grief (emotional shock, denial, anger, remorse, grief, and reconciliation) as the news of a leader's misconduct becomes public. Group members find it harder to trust one another because trust has been betrayed. Drops in enthusiasm and attendance are also common byproducts of a leader's misconduct.

RELATING TO YOUNG PEOPLE IN A HIGHLY SEXUALIZED SOCIETY

Sex is everywhere in our culture. Movies, television, music, fashion, and relationships are inundated with sex. The young people we work with are at the age where they are discovering and exploring their sexuality. Many people and social forces encourage them to participate in sexual activity at an early age. How a youth leader, pastor, or church volunteer speaks and acts with them will deeply impact their understanding of sexuality.

You and your youth ministry staff have a variety of experiences and backgrounds. How can you speak to them with a unified message that protects them from abuse and sets a godly standard for sex they can learn from you and practice in their own lives?

SET A STANDARD OF BEHAVIOR FOR YOUR YOUTH MINISTRY TEAM

Be specific so there are few misunderstandings. Discuss it together, and hold one another accountable to live by it.

Protect your own life from sexual temptation and the destruction it will bring to you.

Protect the young people God has put under your care.

Here's an example of a written standard of behavior used by

one youth organization. You'll find the same material on the CD with this book. You may want to use it as a starting point for developing a policy for your organization.

STAFF/STUDENT APPROPRIATE CONDUCT STANDARDS

The "Two Adult" Meeting Rule

Make every effort to have **two adult leaders** present when interacting with one or more teens. As a general rule, these adults should not be related family members.

One-on-One Meetings of a Leader and Student

At times, having two adults present will not be possible. When this occurs, the following is recommended:

- Notify parents and obtain approval from one parent or guardian whenever practical.

- Try to meet in a public place.

- Meet during the daytime and avoid late-night meetings whenever possible.

- Follow all guidelines given by the parent(s).

Open Door Counseling

During a ministry counseling session, the best practice is to keep the door of the room open for the entire session. Ideally, the session will be conducted at a time when others are nearby. It is best to counsel while in a ministry group setting where witnesses to the conversation are present.

In a formal counseling session where confidentiality is needed, however, the door to the counseling room should have a window. The counselor should face the door and should be easily visible through the window.

The "Three Person" Transportation Rule

We understand that adults may need to drive youth to and from activities. Please make every effort to have a third person in the vehicle. Try to avoid having one young person and one adult of opposite genders in the car alone. If you make any unplanned extra stops, please notify parents if possible.

Sleepover Guidelines

- Signed permission slips must be obtained from at least one parent or guardian.

- The "Two Adult" rule needs to be followed. Two screened adult leaders must be present with up to sixteen (16) students. An extra leader must be included with seventeen (17) or more students, and you should always have a leader-to-student ratio of no less than one leader to eight students.

- The sleepover must be cleared through the Executive Director.

- As long as any students are awake, one of the leaders must also be awake to ensure monitoring of safe behavior.

- Separate sleeping quarters must be designated for males and females.

- Adults cannot share the same bed as a student.

- Don't change clothes in view of students.

- Appropriate modest sleeping attire must be worn.

- Information sheet regarding emergencies must be obtained to and from the parent(s), including the phone numbers and the locations where parents and students can be reached.

- Leaders should check with parents and use good judgment regarding PG or PG-13 movies—no R-rated movies.

- Don't allow students into the master bedroom.

Appropriate Displays of Affection between Adults and Youth:

- Side hugs
- Shoulder-to-shoulder or "temple" hugs
- Pats on the shoulder or back
- Handshakes
- "High-fives"
- Pats on the head when culturally appropriate
- Touching hands, faces, shoulders, and arms
- Arms around shoulders

Inappropriate Displays of Affection:

- Full frontal hugs
- Kisses on the mouth
- Touching bottoms, chests, or genital areas
- Showing affection in isolated areas of a building, such as closets, staff only areas, or other private rooms
- Staff sleeping in bed with a student
- Touching knees or legs
- Male/female and/or one-on-one wrestling
- Piggyback rides
- Tickling
- Any type of massage given by a student to a staff
- Any type of massage given by a staff to a student
- Any form of affection that is unwanted by the student or the staff

Appropriate Verbal Interaction:

- Positive reinforcement
- Appropriate jokes

- Encouragement
- Praise

Inappropriate Verbal Interaction:

- Name Calling
- Adults having sexually oriented conversations with opposite sex teens
- Involving adults or youth in the personal problems or issues of employees or volunteers
- Having secret elements of a relationship with students
- Giving compliments that relate to physique or body development
- Cursing
- Telling off-color or sexualized jokes
- Making comments meant to shame a student
- Belittling
- Making derogatory remarks about an adult, a young person, or a person's family
- Using harsh language that may frighten, threaten, or humiliate students

WRITING YOUR STANDARDS OF BEHAVIOR

Use this example as a guide for your church or youth organization when writing your own standards of behavior. Let your leaders and volunteers know what is expected of them. Be specific. Share these standards with every person who joins your youth ministry team. Review these standards with all team members each year so the entire team can renew their commitment to live by them.

DEVELOPING A COMPREHENSIVE SEXUAL ABUSE POLICY

In addition to established standards of behavior for its employees, every church and organization should also have a comprehensive policy regarding sexual abuse.

DETECTING STAFF MISCONDUCT

Your youth ministry is loaded with sexually charged men and women—both teens and adults. We are all sexual beings who seek to live by God's standards, and we've been given the opportunity to bring others to know true freedom in Christ. When we are tempted, God will help us do what is right. He wants us to help one another with encouragement and accountability. We need to be watching out for situations that can lead us into trouble.

Here are some signs that may indicate inappropriate sexual conduct between adults and youth:

- An adult leader spending time alone with the same young person regularly.

- Frequent physical contact between adult leaders and students (such as touching or hugging).

- A teen becoming more and more dependent on one particular adult leader.

- A teen not mixing with other staff equally.

CRY RAPE

"He tried to rape me in the car on the way here," Denise shouted as she entered the living room. She pointed her finger at Gary, one of our best volunteers. His face turned an ashen white.

"He did not!" countered Jennifer, who was 10 steps behind Denise. "I was in the back seat the whole time. He didn't do nothing."

The color returned to Gary's face. Everybody laughed. Denise had made her first joke of the night.

But what if Jennifer hadn't been in the back seat? Denise was the kind of girl who loved attention and regularly bent the truth to serve her own purposes. Accused without a witness, Gary might not have stood a chance.

We wised up! None of our male staff drove any females alone to any of our meetings the rest of the year.

- An adult leader and a teen giving each other unusual gifts.

- The way the two people in question look at each other.

- What the friends of the teen and adult say or imply about their relationship.

- Reduced involvement of the adult leader's spouse in youth ministry.

- A teen reducing involvement in regular youth program but still showing up before and after activities to see a particular leader.

- A staff member or volunteer consistently giving rides to the same teen and resisting the offer of another staff member to do so.

- A staff member or volunteer going date-type places with a student outside of youth activities.

- An adult leader treating one particular teen to food, tickets, etc.

- A teen becoming extremely emotional without apparent cause.

- A defensive attitude or questioning of behavior standards by the adult leader when the subject of possible misconduct is raised.

- Open defiance of a written standard of behavior by the staff member or volunteer, and minimizing of action when confronted.

CAN YOU ALWAYS DETECT SEXUAL MISCONDUCT?

None of these signs should be taken alone as proof of sexual misconduct. These are only signals that may indicate a possible problem. The more signs present, the stronger your suspicions should be.

Remind your staff that they are expected to live up to the standards of behavior they have signed. Those who refuse to follow the standards should not be permitted to continue working with young people—even if you have no reason to suspect they've been involved in sexual misconduct. This sends a strong message to your entire youth ministry team that you are serious about the standards.

Staff members need regular supervision to help them do their job in the youth ministry. Utilize a balance of group meetings and individual appointments. Use these times to address any concerns you have about how the staff person is relating (positively or negatively) to any of the students. Don't be afraid to openly ask staff if they are having any attractions or feelings toward the students. Give them opportunities to discuss situations that might lead to trouble, so these situations can be addressed before harm is done.

DISCOVERING BAD NEWS

If at any point you discover evidence that a ministry leader is sexually abusing a young person, or if there is an accusation of sexual abuse, you *must* alert the leaders of your church or organization. Don't try to handle an accusation of sexual abuse by yourself or in secret. Workers (paid and volunteer) should take their concerns and evidence to the people in charge of the church or ministry.

If there is conclusive evidence of sexual abuse, those in charge of the ministry or organization should call the police; in fact, contacting the legal authorities in the event of any accusation of sexual abuse is legally mandatory in some states. This call should be made by the persons who are legally responsible for the organization, after consulting the youth ministry team that presented the accusation or evidence.

Every church or organization needs a clear and comprehensive sexual abuse policy that includes a predetermined process to follow to determine the credibility of the accusation and what must be done. Your church leadership board needs to develop and own this process.

You must be confidential and discreet with all information until the matter is settled. Keep written records of all conversations in which any situation involving possible sexual misconduct is discussed. Be as detailed and specific as possible. Talk to your supervisor (senior pastor, elder, director) throughout this process. Ask for their guidance and keep them informed.

Follow the process. If the accusation is false, the truth will be revealed. If it is true, then you must face the truth and take the long-term action to help heal the victim and bring justice and restoration to the offender. It is never fun.

An effective sexual abuse policy starts at the top in your church or youth organization and must be applied to all the age groupings and groups that exist in your ministry. Several outstanding organizations provide training for churches that need to develop a child sexual abuse policy. I recommend that you and other leaders in your church or youth organization attend one of these comprehensive trainings. You will find it thorough, informative, and helpful. Churches can also get guidance from their insurance carrier or lawyer. Another great source is *Reducing the Risk II* written by James Cobble, Richard Hammar, and Steven W. Klipowitz (reducingtherisk. com). This is a product of the Church Law Today organization (www. Churchlawtoday.com).

AN OUNCE OF PREVENTION

The possibility of misconduct should motivate you to screen and supervise diligently. Though it will be time-consuming, it is worth every effort to keep abuse out of your youth ministry. A staff member betraying a young person's trust does enormous damage to people and the ministry while draining emotional energy and enthusiasm from the youth ministry team. Dealing with problems after they occur takes far more time than taking measures to prevent them.

People make the difference. Two different churches in the same denomination may have the same operations manuals and resources yet produce entirely different results. A church develops a good or bad reputation in a community depending on the quality of the leadership. Building a good staff team and training them to work together is essential to a safe youth program.

ARE YOU A SEX ABUSER?

It's possible that you're reading these words knowing there's a secret that *you* have been hiding. Right now or at some time in the past you've been involved in some kind of romantic or sexual relationship with a student in your youth ministry. If that's true—keep reading.

How long can you keep this secret? It's not a question of *if* you'll be discovered; it is only a matter of *when* everyone finds out. Perhaps you feel powerless to change or maybe you're just terrified of the consequences if you tell the truth. You keep hoping time will pass and it will all just go away.

You won't break the domination of this secret or this ongoing immoral relationship until you confess your situation to a trusted leader. That's the first step to breaking free. The consequences will be painful; but if you wait until you are exposed by another person, the consequences will be much more severe. If you wait until someone else exposes your secret, your repentance and remorse will always be questioned because you didn't come forward. People will find it even harder to trust you again.

Don't keep this a secret anymore. You will never feel any relief until you go with your trusted confessor to the person under whose authority you minister. Pray together and ask that person to help you map out plans designed to repair the damage done to others and restore your integrity.

OR DO YOU JUST FANTASIZE?

Do you ever fantasize about sexual encounters with students in your youth ministry? The talk shows may say it's healthy; Jesus says it's just like committing adultery (Matthew 5:28). According to James 1:14–15, such thinking is a step on the road to actually doing it.

Fantasizing is a difficult habit to break. But try this: The next time you engage in some kind of sexual thoughts about a young person in your ministry, be sure to keep fantasizing all the way to the end of the story. Don't stop when you reach the steamy parts. Keep going and imagine what you will say to that person 10 minutes after it's over. What will you say when you find out she is pregnant or he's told his best friend about you? Fantasize about how you'll feel when your spouse or best friend finds out. Picture the scene when you tell your own children. Picture how you'll feel leading the youth group when you suspect some of them have heard a rumor about you? Fantasize the whole deal. Now that you see the whole picture, how does that little sexual fantasy feel?

REPORTING SEXUAL ABUSE AND PHYSICAL ABUSE

When students trust you and feel secure in your youth ministry, they will tell you some of the secrets of their lives. Be prepared. Hearing what is actually going on in some homes can be shocking.

If a young person gives you reason to believe physical or sexual abuse is occurring, you must take action. Every paid or volunteer staff member must report all suspicions of sexual or physical abuse to the head of the youth ministry. The head of the youth ministry should discuss these reports immediately with the pastor of the church or director of the organization. This should all be done quickly and confidentially.

In many states the professional youth worker or pastor has been designated a mandated reporter who is required by law to report any allegations of abuse to a hotline run by the state government. Check the regulations of your state and comply with them. Often there is a mandated time period (24 to 48 hours) in which youth workers must report what they have discovered. Learn the process and system in your state.

The first time I called the sexual abuse hotline, I agonized over my decision. A 16-year-old girl had told one of our female volunteers that her stepfather was coming into her room at night and sexually touching her. When the volunteer told me, I was shocked. This was an active church family. Everything about this family looked great on the outside.

We sent one of our female staff workers with the volunteer to talk with the girl to confirm what she'd said. The staff worker then reported the girl's allegations to me. As the director of the program, I knew the law required me to make the call. But I was afraid of how the state agency would respond and what would happen to everyone involved. I knew my call would set off a chain reaction that would forever alter the lives of these people.

I called the sexual abuse hotline. I was impressed with how much care and time the state agency took with my report and my concerns about the family. I realize that state agencies mishandle some situations and that the quality of the response depends on the person assigned to the case, but I found some good people waiting at the other end of the line to help. They responded immediately by contacting the young woman at school and the parents when they arrived home from work. The mother admitted she'd had suspicions but had been afraid to confront her husband. The stepfather agreed to undergo counseling. The young woman was taken out of the home and placed with her grandmother several miles away.

Many issues still face each person in that family, but our action brought about significant positive change in that young woman's life. She hated us for a few weeks after we reported it. That was hard on all of us, especially the volunteer she'd told initially. Several months later, however, she expressed gratitude that we'd acted and that she was not being abused anymore.

REFLECT AND INTERACT

Stop and reflect on your experiences and decisions related to the safety of young people. Better yet, discuss these questions with your youth ministry team:

- How have issues of sexual misconduct or abuse touched your life personally?

- What sexual temptations do you experience? How do you keep yourself from seeing a young person as a sexual object?

- In what ways are you "feeding" purity or impurity in your mind and heart?

- How can standards of appropriate and inappropriate behavior with young people help a youth ministry team avoid sexual misconduct?

STAFF SELECTION

When Joe arrived from another state and became the new youth pastor, he seemed like an answer to prayer. The church had gone a long time without a full-time youth pastor. Everyone was impressed by Joe's charisma and enthusiasm for spending time with the youth of the church. He seemed like the ideal youth leader in every way.

What a shock two years later when a middle school boy told his former Sunday school teacher that Joe had touched him sexually. The teacher brought the allegation to the pastor. At first the pastor was sure the boy was lying. Joe denied the charges, and the boy and his family were emotionally and socially ostracized from the church community.

A month later another boy came forward with a similar story. Then another and another, until six boys were reporting that the youth leader had seduced them. Over the next few months, I watched that church get torn apart by the discovery that their youth pastor had been molesting boys in the youth group.

The pastor and the church board had a short meeting with Joe and dismissed him. He disappeared quickly. When the pastor called his out-of-state friend who had recommended Joe, he discovered stories about Joe had surfaced in that community after he had left. People had chosen not to say anything because nobody knew if the rumors were true. Joe seemed like such a nice guy and was so good with kids.

STAFF SELECTION AND SUPERVISION

A staff leader's mistakes can cause tremendous damage to a church, its young people, and their families. It's just common sense to go to great lengths to select the right staff and eliminate the potential sexual violators.

During the last 20 years the number of civil suit awards related to employee misconduct has increased 3,000 percent. The amount of money awarded in those lawsuits has increased 5,000 percent. More important than the money and the legal problems is the damage that's been done to young people.

In light of what is at stake, every youth ministry should reexamine its process of accepting and employing leaders (both paid and volunteer) to be sure that reasonable precautions are taken to screen out potential offenders.

Screening and background checks are now standard procedure with churches and youth organizations aware of the danger of sexual abusers and predators. These groups recognize their responsibility to protect the children and youth under their care. The screening process must be consistent, with an established standard of investigation for each level of leadership involvement. That standard should be applied equally, without discrimination, to every individual seeking to be involved in the ministry. Being a longtime member of the church, a church officer, or a friend of the pastor does not exclude a person from the necessary review.

No process is fool proof. But every church and organization must take reasonable and consistent steps to obtain information that would reveal any past behavior that might predict potentially dangerous behavior by an employee or volunteer.

SCREENING POTENTIAL STAFF (PAID AND VOLUNTEER)

I recommend the following steps in recruiting youth ministry staff.

A WRITTEN APPLICATION

I will limit my comments about the application process to safety-related matters. Obviously, the application can also request information concerning a wide area of topics such as interests, spiritual experiences, beliefs, and previous experience working with children or youth.

Regarding safety matters, the application should ask about a person's education and employment records and should request phone numbers where past schooling and employment can be confirmed. Any gaps in employment or education are cause for asking additional questions about the period of time in question.

On the application include these questions:

- Have you ever been charged with, pled guilty or no contest to, or been convicted of any criminal violation or any type of sexual misconduct or abuse concerning a minor? If yes, please explain.

- Have you ever pled guilty or no contest to, or been convicted of any other criminal offense (misdemeanor or felony, other than a parking violation) in a court of law? If yes, please provide date(s), location(s) and violation(s).

- Have you ever been disciplined, suspended, or terminated by any organization due to allegations of any type of sexual misconduct or abuse? If yes, please explain.

Conclude the application with a statement for the person to sign and date: "I testify that my answers to the above questions are complete and truthful." Consult with your local legal counsel to be sure the application questions are legal in your state.

Requesting this information on the application will help screen out potential offenders who might harm your kids and will also protect your youth ministry from charges that you knowingly employed someone with a record of abusive behavior. Obviously, the applicant can lie. But if you had no reason to suspect the applicant wasn't telling the truth, a jury will find difficulty in holding you responsible for involving the person in your program. If you have reason to suspect the information the applicant provides is not truthful, it is your responsibility to probe more deeply until you are satisfied that you know the truth.

BACKGROUND CHECKS

The process of conducting background checks varies from state to state. Doing these checks is getting easier. Some good companies now provide this service for a reasonable price. Denominations and organizations can greatly reduce the cost by making arrangements for all the churches or groups involved. The background check is a strong statement to parents and your community that you are serious about protecting their children from potential abusers. It also sends a clear message to your applicant that you are serious about finding out the truth.

The type of background check you order can vary with the type of contact the volunteer is expected to have with children and youth. A criminal records check is recommended for all volunteers who will have frequent, unsupervised access to children and youth. The criminal records check may not be appropriate for volunteers who will be in contact with children and youth infrequently or only in settings with multiple adults present (like an event).

Most applicants you encounter probably will not have criminal records. When you do find something, however, the content is usually significant. When a background check turns up information about

COMMON MISTAKES IN VOLUNTEER RECRUITMENT

- We avoid recruiting mature volunteers. We overlook people who have years of experience because we think a volunteer has to be young to relate to teenagers.

- We sign up and employ volunteers too quickly without thorough screening and orientation.

- We are overloaded with young, single college guys who have a natural sexual attraction to the girls in the group. Most guys mean well but aren't trained by leaders to understand the forces at work or the temptations they will face.

- We recruit too few women, and those who are involved are too often placed in non-leadership positions. Women tend to be more safety-conscious than men and have plenty to offer when events and activities are being planned.

an accusation or conviction for sex abuse or molestation in the past, you must discuss this with the applicant. Some people freely admit to these prior incidents but explain that their subsequent religious conversion has put all that in the past. Are they still a risk to children? Tough question. You shouldn't doubt the sincerity of anyone's religious conversion, but I don't think there is adequate evidence from a legal standpoint to trust these individuals to work with children again. Don't put them in positions that work with children or youth. It is too much of a risk. Find another ministry in the church where they can get involved, away from children and youth.

Driving records are easy to obtain and relevant for any staff who will be driving vehicles as part of their ministry responsibilities. If a potential volunteer will be driving teens as part of ministry involvement, a motor vehicle records check is absolutely necessary.

All records you request and obtain must be kept confidential and locked in files where no unauthorized person has access. The content of these reports cannot be talked about with anyone outside your selection committee.

Sometimes just asking for permission to do a background check will cause a person to withdraw from the application process. You don't need to know the details or pursue the matter further. You have your answer—that person doesn't belong on the youth ministry team. When you do check records, your policy and practice must be consistently applied to every applicant. You could be sued for discrimination if you treat one applicant differently than another.

REFERENCES

Ask the applicant to provide two references from personal contacts and two from work situations. If he or she has worked or volunteered in other positions with children and youth, be sure to get a reference from supervisors from that group. You should also request a reference from a pastor or leader in the church who knows the person well. Design the reference response form to meet your specific ministry situation. It helps the person writing the reference to know the job for which the friend is applying. Give a brief description of your ministry and what you are asking this applicant to do in the ministry.

Ask questions that will give you insight into the person's personality and behavior patterns, as well as his or her skills and abilities.

If you have questions after reading a reference form (or if a form is not returned), take the initiative to call the person for additional information or clarification. Ask the hard questions directly and without embarrassment. Give the person the opportunity to talk with you directly about something he or she might feel uncomfortable writing. Don't shortcut the reference process. You may obtain information from a reference source you couldn't get from anyone else, which could be key to really knowing the applicant.

PERSONAL INTERVIEW

Ideally each applicant should have separate interviews with two different people—at least one of which should be done by someone who does not know the applicant well. (Interviewing someone you know well seldom turns up any new information.) Conduct a standard interview with all applicants, asking each person a set of predetermined questions.

Find a professional who interviews job applicants and work with this person to develop questions that will help you gain the information you need from your interviews. You will want to know the applicants' expectations and reasons for being involved, their attitudes toward teenagers, their relational skills, their ability to handle conflicts and crises, their special abilities, their legal or criminal histories, and their spiritual commitments to Christ. Take notes during the meeting, and after the interview write out the details of what you heard.

FINAL DECISION

Work with a team of people (leaders in your church or organization) to make a determination on the applicants. It will be more objective when the people who handle the written information (application and references) are different from those who conduct interviews. The final decision should include members of the leadership team who know the applicant well and those who don't. Let each person on the team share his or her particular perspective on the applicant.

From a safety standpoint a qualified youth ministry team member should demonstrate the following:

- responsibility
- decision-making ability
- good judgment
- trustworthiness
- willingness to follow instructions and safety guidelines
- willingness to follow standards of behavior and interaction with youth

Any inconsistencies of the applicant will become more readily apparent when discussed in a varied group. By using this information and taking time for prayer, the group can make a wise decision about each applicant's fitness for involvement on the youth ministry team and the areas of training and growth needed.

NO SHORTCUTS

This screening process is lengthy, but it protects you in several vital areas. It eliminates people who are only partially committed. (You would have discovered that limited commitment during the first six months of the person's service.) The process also gives you more confidence that the accepted applicant will not hurt the kids you care so much about. The person can still disappoint you, but you will know it was his or her doing, not your carelessness, that hurt the kids. This process will also serve you well if you are called to defend it in a legal proceeding. It will be clear that you took the precautions a reasonable person would expect.

Volunteers are so hard to find that none of us wants to place any hindrances or roadblocks in their way. At first glance this application system seems more of a deterrent than an incentive to volunteer recruitment. During my ministry in Youth for Christ, I confess that I've often chosen the shortcut and placed people in the ministry who were safety risks to our most precious commodity—our young people. I have learned the hard way that poor decisions always come back to hurt you.

Having high standards for acceptance as a youth ministry team member can be a positive public relations spin for you. Parents and community people who hear about your stringent volunteer standards will view your youth ministry as responsible and trustworthy.

TRAINING YOUR MINISTRY STAFF

Selecting the right people is only the beginning. You must also prepare them to work effectively with young people. No one can predict every situation your staff will encounter in youth ministry. Your job is to help them grow and be ready for the challenges they will face with young people.

Maintain records of all your staff meetings and training sessions. Keep a folder on file for each staff member with their application, references, any notes from supervision meetings, and a record of the training he or she has completed.

When an accident or an act of misconduct puts the spotlight of scrutiny on your ministry, investigators will check the appropriateness of the staff you've chosen to employ. They will also check the training you've provided to prepare your staff to do their jobs. This section on training will again focus specifically on the safety aspect of your curriculum.

Your staff training should include these facets:

ORIENTATION SESSION

Volunteers need a two-to-ten-hour basic training and orientation to the ministry. They need to know how the organization works and their role in it.

TRAINING ON APPROPRIATE AND INAPPROPRIATE INTERACTIONS WITH YOUTH

Read and discuss a specific list describing what is allowed and not allowed. (See chapter 5 for more on this.) Have staff and volunteers sign the list as a pledge to follow the rules.

FIRST AID TRAINING

A certain number of staff members will need to complete a certified first aid training course. The remaining staff can take a simplified first aid course to learn the basics. Enough staff should be certified to make sure every event can have a trained, certified staff person in attendance.

IDENTIFYING CHILD AND SEXUAL ABUSE

All staff members need training to learn to recognize the signs of abuse and how to report it within the organization so the mandated reporter can inform the proper authorities. You can find instructors at a local college or within a local child-service or protection agency.

SUICIDE PREVENTION TRAINING

Find a social worker who can help train you and your staff to respond to suicide threats made by teenagers.

CRISIS INTERVENTION TRAINING

If staff members are building relationships with kids, they will witness many crises. This training will help them recognize when they are in situations that are over their heads and help them know how to get professional help.

PREGNANCY, DRUG ABUSE, AND AIDS TRAINING

These conditions touch more teenagers each year. Some staff or volunteers should pursue additional training to specialize in these social problems.

ACTIVITY TRAINING

This includes training to cover specific activities and events held by the youth ministry (such as canoeing, biking, or backpacking).

REFLECT AND INTERACT

Stop and reflect on your experiences and decisions related to the safety of young people. Better yet, discuss these questions with your youth ministry team:

- What is your organization's process for selecting and training new staff? How could it be made more effective?

- Is a background check a standard part of your procedure in evaluating every potential staff member or volunteer?

- What concerns do you have about a more vigorous safety policy with regard to volunteers?

BUSES, VANS, AND AUTOMOBILES

The plan was perfect. Brian was sure he could beat the crowds and get home early for a full Sunday with the family. His youth group had been among the crowd of 25,000 at a giant, Christian music festival Friday night and all day Saturday. The big finale was Saturday at midnight. Most people pack up and leave on Sunday morning. The traffic jam tests the patience of even the strongest Christians. Brian's group never gets an early start—try waking up kids early on Sunday morning. Nearly impossible. On top of that they have at least a six-hour drive home.

Brian's plan was simple. Pack up the vans and leave after the midnight finale. The kids will sleep all the way home. They will miss the traffic and get home early enough to spend Sunday with their families, not on the road.

Brian's perfect plan went bad around 4 a.m. when the lead van veered across the center median, crossed the oncoming traffic miraculously without hitting an oncoming car, and rolled over as it hit the ditch on the side of the road. The driver had fallen asleep.

Several kids and adult leaders went to the hospital. Within a week everybody was out and doing better. Thank God.

They dodged a big bullet, but Brian still felt responsible. His desire to get home and avoid the Sunday morning crowds blocked out the reality that his drivers weren't rested enough for an all-night run. They'd spent the entire day out in the sun enjoying the music with everyone else. He'd put his whole group in danger because he wanted a quick, hassle-free trip home. How would he have lived with himself if someone had been killed?

The results weren't as forgiving for a New York church transporting students to a conference in North Carolina. The 22-year-old driver mistakenly steered the 6000-pound, 15-passenger van onto the right shoulder of a rural highway near the end of their long trip. When he tried to steer back onto the roadway, he overcorrected and lost control. The van rolled over three times, ejecting eight of its nine passengers. One young man died. Five others were hospitalized. The circumstances included several factors common to rollover accidents—a young driver, a loaded tall van, and a rural road. So sad.

GUILTY

That's how most of us in youth ministry have to plead when charged with violations of safety involving buses, vans, and automobiles. These extreme examples of safety violations reveal the danger involved when we mix young people, vehicles, and leaders who ignore safety issues.

Everybody has a story. While interviewing youth workers for this book, the issues of vehicles and safety came up more often than any other subject. Most youth workers admit overloading vehicles with too many people, breaking the speed limit, not using seatbelts, and committing other offenses for which police routinely write tickets. Many also raised concerns about the qualifications of the people whom they call upon to drive for their events and the mechanical condition of the vehicles they use.

Transportation is the second biggest danger in youth ministry. Safety violations and shortcomings make the average church and youth ministry organization quite vulnerable to tragic accidents and lawsuits.

TIME TO GET ORGANIZED

An increasing number of churches are recognizing the need for a transportation committee to set policy and monitor drivers and vehicles. A typical committee would consist of four to six people with representation from the pastoral staff, church officers, parents, and youth ministry staff.

The first task of a church transportation committee is to produce a written policy statement establishing ground rules for operating the vehicles used for ministry purposes. The committee should meet frequently until such a policy is created. Once these ground rules are in place, meetings can be conducted quarterly.

The written policy statement should address the use of any church-owned vehicles (specifying who uses them for what purposes); a process for designating qualified drivers; a list of responsibilities of drivers before, during, and after trips; and written assignments for those responsible for maintenance and upkeep.

An additional policy should be established for the ministry-related use of personal vehicles owned and operated by parents and volunteers. Such a policy would include a standard of qualifications for potential drivers in the ministry, so that no student is ever placed with an unsafe driver.

> On the CD included with this book, you'll find a sample policy for ministry vehicles that can be adjusted to suit your circumstances.

WHO CAN DRIVE?

Drivers need to meet several key qualifications.

ACCEPTABLE AGE

Each driver should be at least 21 years old. Some insurance companies require drivers to be 25. Check with your insurance agent.

DRIVING RECORD

Each driver's record should be checked for traffic violations and accident records. The committee should consult with an insurance company to decide what constitutes a satisfactory record.

PERSONAL INSURANCE COVERAGE

The committee should know the amount of liability insurance each driver carries on his or her personal policy. It is wise to set a minimum level of coverage required to be a driver for the youth ministry.

AGREEMENT TO SAFE DRIVING STANDARDS

The committee should provide a written statement describing responsible driving. Each driver should read and sign the statement, which is kept on file by the committee. Drivers who violate the agreed standard must be confronted, and the violations corrected.

HELPING DRIVERS DO THEIR BEST

Drivers are special volunteers who deserve quality treatment. Volunteer drivers need the careful support of the youth ministry leader so they can do their best.

WRITTEN DIRECTIONS AND INFORMATION

Every driver needs written directions to the destination (including a map and phone number). On longer trips drivers should be given any money needed for gas or tolls and any special instructions about the trip (for example, planned stops to eat and use the restrooms).

ADULT SUPPORT

Depending on the length of the trip, each driver may need another capable adult driver traveling with him or her. Assistance is needed to share driving, handle directions, and deal with any distractions in the vehicle. Expecting leaders to drive home after a tiring weekend in which they've had limited sleep puts the youth in that vehicle at risk. A reasonable alternative is to bring on the trip qualified adults whose main responsibilities are to drive, serve as support staff, and stay well rested for the trip home. The extra drivers also serve as backups in case any leader is injured or becomes ill and cannot drive home.

TRIAL RUN

Prior to the trip make sure every driver has a practice run in the vehicle he or she will drive. Driving a van or pulling a trailer is much different than driving a passenger car. Give adequate opportunity for the driver to practice tight turns, parking, braking, and backing up. Be sure the mirrors are positioned properly and the seat adjusted for easy operation of the pedals. Your drivers need to feel comfortable and confident to do their best job for your youth program.

EMERGENCY PLAN

Before the trip begins, discuss with all drivers your instructions for communicating with other drivers during the trip and handling emergencies. Does each driver have the cell phone numbers of the other drivers in case someone needs to stop or gets separated from the group? How should they handle bad weather or poor driving conditions? After discussing the possible difficulties, the leader and the drivers can spend some time together in prayer asking God to help them as they serve.

CARAVANNING

This almost universal method of transporting a youth group to a weekend retreat can be a nightmare if you don't prepare all the drivers to follow these few basic rules:

- Use specific written directions. Each driver should be able to tell his passengers when the food and restroom stops will be happening.

- Agree on a distress signal or how you will use cell phones to communicate in case of a problem.

- Talk through what a driver should do if the vehicle becomes separated from the group.

WHAT AM I DOING?

"Every Thursday after gym night at a local school, we would pack all the kids into the church van for the 10-minute ride back to the church. Since we were always hot and sweaty, a special tradition evolved. We drove with the side door open.

"As the attendance grew and the van became more crowded, the brave ones stood in the open doorway with their faces in the wind like dogs riding with the car windows down. One night I hit the brakes suddenly as we entered the church parking lot to avoid hitting a cat. Three of the guys were launched right out the door and onto the pavement. They hit, rolled, and popped up laughing. Everyone in the van cheered and laughed.

"Later that night after everyone had gone home, I prayed and thanked God for protecting those three young men. Driving home I asked God to forgive me for being so stupid and to give me the courage to close that side door next week and keep it closed."

Mike, youth pastor from Michigan

- Avoid changing lanes excessively. The driver of the lead vehicle should be thoughtful of the whole caravan when changing lanes, making turns, and going through traffic lights. All cars should use turn signals to alert the caravan to turns and lane changes.

- No competing or socializing while cars are on the highway.

FOLLOW THE EXAMPLE

The staff leader sets the pace. Volunteers need to see the one who makes the rules living by those same rules. Uniform observance of speed limits, seatbelt requirements, limited use of cell phones, and other guidelines is way leaders demonstrate unity before the students.

STUDENT DRIVERS

You won't find many insurance agents approving of high school students driving for youth group activities. You shouldn't either. We put our teens and ourselves at great risk when we let teenagers drive.

Most of us have felt the pressure of teens who wants to drive for us. They play on our emotions. (Don't we trust them?) They offer to solve our immediate problems. (We didn't plan for enough drivers!) It is tempting. Having a clear written policy about qualified drivers takes the pressure off of us. We are protected by the written rules of the church or organization.

How do you handle the student who insists on driving? You can't stop him or her from personally driving to your events or meetings. You should discuss the young person's request to drive with his or her parent(s). If the student is determined to drive his or her car to an outside event, instruct the student to meet you at your destination, not at your departure point. No students under your supervision should ride with the teen driver at any time. If he or she is driving friends to the meetings, take the initiative and talk to all the parents involved, informing them of your policy and their responsibility if they permit their teens to ride with the young driver.

VEHICLE SAFETY

Reliable vehicles are just as important as qualified drivers in the quest for safe transportation. Failure to provide or maintain quality vehicles for transporting students can be the primary reason for a tragic accident and the basis of a liability judgment against your youth ministry.

A youth pastor in New York is thankful his church started using the youth ministry van during the day to help with the nursery school and daycare. The state requires a mandatory vehicle inspection every six months for vans used in nursery school operations. Problems and dangerous situations are now fixed immediately. The vans have never been in better shape.

Don't wait for your state to enact similar strict regulations. For the safety of the students you love, have your vehicle inspected by a qualified mechanic every six months. Keep good records. This will protect you from accusations of negligence and will alert you to potential problems with brakes, exhaust system, cooling system, and so forth before you face an emergency hundreds of miles from home.

Before any trip (within 24 hours of departure) every vehicle should go through a "pre-flight" check. You don't have to be a mechanic to check if you have:

- Current registration and inspection stickers
- Registration/insurance paperwork required to be carried
- An extra set of keys
- A flashlight
- A first aid kit
- A repair/supply kit (extra oil, wiper fluid, water, basic tools, garbage bags, rags, jumper cables)
- An inflated spare tire and tools for a tire change
- Seatbelts in working order

- Functioning lights and signals

- Wiper blades in good condition

- Snow brush or ice scraper for winter conditions.

Looking under the hood:

- Are belts tight? Are any frayed or brittle? It's always smart to carry an extra set. You always seem to need them when auto parts stores are closed.

- How are the oil, transmission, radiator, and brake fluid levels?

- Are the battery terminals clean and the wires in good shape?

- Are the radiator hoses in good shape?

- Is the air conditioning functioning properly?

- Are the tires properly inflated, without any gashes or bubbles?

- What about the lights and tire inflation on the trailer?

A member of the transportation committee who is solid in basic mechanics can play a key role helping you inspect each vehicle before each trip. Having someone see you off before each trip with a vehicle check can be a special ministry. It will take pressure off the leader's mind to know each vehicle has been cleared for takeoff. Prepare a checklist that can be used for each vehicle. The inspector can keep a written record of the precautions you've taken to provide safe transportation.

PROTECTING THE MINISTRY-OWNED VEHICLE

While every volunteer vehicle should be treated with the highest care, vehicles owned by the church or youth ministry require special stewardship. When a vehicle is used by multiple drivers, accurate records are vital. Everyone who signs out and drives your ministry's vehicle should read your basic rules of the road and sign a statement acknowledging acceptance of those standards. It is simple to produce a short sign-out form to be completed each time the vehicle is used. (A sample form is included as part of the transportation policy on the accompanying CD.)

When returning the vehicle, drivers should make note of any problems they encountered while using the vehicle. Immediate attention can be given to body damage, mechanical problems, or reports of noises in the engine. Requiring vehicles to be cleaned inside and outside when they are returned lengthens their life of service to the ministry. People treat clean vehicles with more care and caution. A dirty, cluttered vehicle triggers an attitude of thoughtless abuse by students and adults.

BASIC SAFETY STANDARDS

Every vehicle used in ministry should meet these standards:

ASLEEP AT THE WHEEL: THREE SNAPSHOTS

"I can't believe how foolish we were for many years driving all through the night taking kids to camp in Colorado. Many nights I was half asleep and fighting it as the van full of sleeping teenagers raced down the road through the darkness. Now that I am a parent, I realize how carelessly we were hauling that precious cargo."

Gary, youth worker from Minnesota

"The youth leader never sleeps. I'm tired before the retreat even starts. Then two nights of little sleep followed by the trip home…and I'm driving. That can't be safe for my kids. I know how exhausted I am. Next trip I will have special designated drivers."

Mike, youth pastor from New Jersey

"Five years ago I fell asleep driving a jeep full of teens home from a snow camp. Fortunately, the snow was piled high along the shoulder of the road. When we hit the bank of snow it caught the vehicle and kept us from crashing. I was wiped out after two days of skiing and leading the youth program. The students later told me that as I was driving and dozing, they kept asking me if I was okay. I kept telling them I was fine when, in reality, I could hardly keep my eyes open. I am so grateful to God for sparing me from what could have been an awful tragedy. I don't take chances now."

Clayton, pastor from New York

- The vehicle should not be overloaded. Have a legal limit clearly marked on the sign-out sheet.

- Every person should have a seat and should use a seatbelt when the vehicle is in motion. This is required for front and back seats. No sitting on the floor or on the laps of other people. (Some people may feel using seat belts at all times is annoying, but it is the only smart choice to make. In accidents the risk of serious injury is much greater for those who are not belted in.)

- No doors are to be opened when the vehicle is in motion. All doors should be locked. No body parts should be protruding out of the windows.

- No students are to leave the vehicle while on the roadway stopped in traffic or at a traffic signal. (This means no "Chinese fire drills" or similar stunts.)

- No passenger should hinder or distract the driver while the vehicle is in motion.

- When the vehicle stops, no passenger should exit until either the engine is turned off or the driver gives specific verbal permission.

- When stopping to eat or use restrooms, speak to all students before they exit the vehicle. Set a time to be back to the vehicle. Warn students about traffic in the parking lot. Caution them about crossing the road to visit another restaurant or store, especially if it is after dark. Be sure to count and confirm everyone's presence before starting the vehicle to leave.

- Nothing should be thrown from the vehicle.

- Luggage (more than 10 pounds) should never be stowed above the height of the seats. In case of an accident or a sudden stop, the luggage becomes a dangerous fast-moving object aimed at the heads and necks of passengers. Luggage should not be stowed where it blocks the side doors of a van in case passengers have to make an emergency exit.

- The drivers should never use a cell phone while the vehicle is in motion. Talking on a cell phone while driving is illegal in some states. Necessary phone communication with other cars should be done by the front seat passenger holding the cell phone and using the speakerphone setting.

INSURANCE

Liability insurance is a top concern for any vehicle owned or used by your youth ministry. The amount of liability coverage you carry is a decision for the governing body of your church or youth organization with the guidance of your insurance carrier.

Personal vehicles with minimal liability insurance should not be driven for youth ministry activities. In most states each volunteer should carry at least $100,000/$300,000 liability coverage ($100,000 maximum per person and $300,000 maximum per incident) plus a $1 million personal liability umbrella policy. In some states and metropolitan areas, higher amounts of coverage are needed. Vehicles (especially vans and buses) owned by the church or youth organization require liability coverage greater than $1 million. In the event of a van or bus accident involving serious injuries and fatalities, $1 million of coverage will be exhausted quickly. Inadequate insurance coverage can seriously damage the assets of individual volunteers and organizations who will be targeted by the lawsuits. Such accidents are traumatic enough without being compounded by financial struggles.

HANDLING BREAKDOWNS

Breakdowns are a gift from God! Young people can learn more about the Christian faith of their leader when the van breaks down on the trip home than they did during all the programs and meetings of the retreat. God gives us opportunities to live out our faith when we are tempted to lose our temper, worry, or curse the lousy bus or van. It's a lesson in real life our kids will never forget.

In the event of a breakdown, after you've thanked God for this great opportunity to demonstrate the Christian faith, you have to deal with the problem. It can be anything from a flat tire to some type of engine trouble. Here's a plan of action:

- Do your best to park in the safest spot you can find away from the flow of traffic. You may be sitting there for a while, so make it the best possible spot you can safely reach.

- Unless you're faced with some imminent danger (such as a fire in the engine or exhaust fumes), keep the students in the vehicle. Be firm. You don't need additional supervision responsibilities at that time.

- Look for the problem and decide how serious it is. If a knowledgeable person is riding with you, ask for help. Discuss together the kind of help you need, and think about where you could obtain it. If you need to call for help, try to determine your location so you can convey it accurately. Remain calm and confident that God will help you through these difficult moments.

- Return to the vehicle and talk with the students. Tell them openly and honestly about the situation. Pray together for God's protection and help. Ask them for their best cooperation and support. It may mean remaining in the vehicle while you try to obtain help or perhaps vacating the vehicle while you jack it up to change a tire. If they leave the vehicle, they should move together to a safe place that you designate and stay there. Most importantly, keep them away from the road.

- Exercise your best option. Use your cell phone to seek help or get advice. You can call the police or information to obtain road repair and assistance.

Here's another place where thoughtful preparations pay dividends. The youth leader needs to carry either a roadside assistance/towing service membership card or a major credit card provided by the church for emergency use. It is also wise to have a transportation committee member on call during this travel time. The member can be praying for you during travel time and also be ready to receive any calls for assistance or advice. The member may want to discuss repairs that need to be made or dispatch a back-up vehicle to come and pick up the stranded passengers. That committee member can also activate a phone chain to alert parents to the probable late return. Planning can provide a helpful voice at the other end of the line that can help share the pressure.

CONFRONTING DANGEROUS SITUATIONS

You never know when you might encounter a dangerous driving situation. So you should be ready, just in case.

IS THE 15-PASSENGER VAN SAFE?

The 15-passenger van has been the vehicle of choice for most churches for many years. In recent years concern has grown about the safety of these vehicles. Between 1990 and 2001, 1,441 of these vans were involved in fatal crashes—including 601 single vehicle wrecks that killed 1,924 people (according to the National Highway Traffic Safety Administration).

Carolyn Brown, a spokesperson for Ford Motor Company, one of several automakers that produce the vans, told *Newsday* in January 2004 that Ford recommends drivers of 15-passenger vans "avoid sharp turns, excessive speeds, and abrupt maneuvers." She added that 15-passenger vans should be operated only by trained, experienced drivers.

Some churches and youth organizations, in consultation with their insurance carriers, have banned the use of the 15-passenger vans for youth ministry activities. Other groups have removed the rear seat of the vans and reduced the capacity to 11 passengers. (Critics argue this does not lessen the risk of a rollover if the rear space is filled with luggage and equipment that equals or exceeds the weight of the passengers who would have been seated there.) Every church and youth ministry organization must seriously consider the safety record of this type of vehicle and consult with insurance agents and legal counsel to determine if it should use a 15-passenger van.

FOGGED OR ICED WINDOWS

Drivers should never drive their vehicles when visibility is poor, so it's essential to keep the front and back windows clear. Drivers cannot make good decisions if they cannot see the traffic coming from all directions. Don't be lazy. Keep the windows clear.

BACKING UP

Fogged windows and impaired vision can make backing out of a parking space dangerous. If the driver isn't sure what is behind the vehicle, he or she should put it in park and get out and take a look. In a tight squeeze the driver could have a responsible student stand behind the vehicle and guide him or her out.

BRAKING TIME AND DISTANCE

Drivers should take time to get adjusted to the brakes of the vehicle they've been asked to drive. Remember that a loaded vehicle takes longer to stop than an empty one. Don't tailgate other vehicles. Allow plenty of space.

BAD WEATHER CONDITIONS

In bad weather, slowing down is imperative. Most accidents are caused by excessive speed for the prevailing road conditions.

FATIGUE

Traveling through the night with only one driver is foolish and dangerous. Provide relief. Make sure your drivers get some sleep before the trip home. Better yet, have designated drivers who will not wear themselves out participating with the students during the trip.

HIRING A PROFESSIONAL BUS COMPANY

Sometimes it's better to leave the driving to someone else. If your staff and volunteers aren't worrying about transportation responsibilities, they can stay more focused on the students and the programming.

If you decide to hire a professional bus company, don't be shy about checking its safety record and reputation. Ask the company for names of other groups they have serviced. Call those groups for recommendations.

Several safety concerns particularly relate to using a professional bus company. Your group should appoint one staff leader as bus captain to serve as liaison with the driver. The bus captain should be your group's communication link with the professional driver throughout the trip.

Ask the professional driver about any safety rules he or she wants enforced during the trip. Most likely the driver will ask people to remain in their seats while the bus is moving. No one should sleep in the overhead storage area or on the floor.

At a rest area, speak to all the students before they exit the bus. Set a time to be back on the bus. Warn students to be careful about traffic in the parking lot or when crossing streets. Be sure to get a head count to confirm everyone's presence before leaving a rest area.

Professional bus drivers are known for their driving skills and savvy. Unfortunately, many of them also drive consistently above the legal limit. If you feel uncomfortable about the speed or any other aspect of the driving, do not hesitate to discuss it with the driver. Express yourself respectfully, but be firm about your safety concerns. You are the customer, so the driver and his company should be trying to please you. Even if your concerns are not warmly received, the driver may be more conscious of safety during the rest of the trip because you spoke out.

If someone becomes ill on the bus, this should be communicated to the driver immediately. The driver can contact police or an ambulance by radio if needed. Each bus should have a first aid kit along with garbage bags, air freshener, and paper towels to clean up any mess. The permission/medical forms should be accessible to the leader, not packed and stored under the bus.

If your group takes a bus to your destination, you may want to rent a car during your time at that location. You may need a vehicle during your stay at a camp or resort to carry any student who might need medical attention.

REFLECT AND INTERACT

Stop and reflect on your experiences and decisions related to the safety of young people. Better yet, discuss these questions with your youth ministry team:

- What accidents or close calls have you had with vehicles on youth ministry trips?

- How prepared and experienced are the people who drive the vehicles carrying your youth ministry kids?

- What vehicle safety standards do you need to start enforcing more diligently?

NO BULLY ZONE

CHAPTER 8

"I was Meatball." The words hung in the air.

Dan, a dynamic 25-year-old youth worker was telling us a piece of his personal story we'd never known. His eyes were a little wet. You could hear the emotion in his voice. "In the seventh grade I was short, round, and fat. When one of the popular kids in the youth group called me 'Meatball,' everybody laughed, and it stuck—like glue. That was my new identity. I started to become what my classmates told me I was. Even now, more than 10 years later I still catch myself thinking like I'm still 'Meatball'—the little fat kid everybody laughs at."

Dan explained how the laughter and ridicule made him dislike himself during his middle school years. Looking at him now—the talented, confident man who leads a creative arts ministry for Youth With a Mission—it's hard to believe.

For Dan the change started when his youth pastor stepped in front of the taunting kids, put his arm around Dan, and called him by his real name. All through his teenage years his youth pastor stood up for him and gave him encouragement and opportunities to develop his talents as well as his faith while his body went through all the developmental changes.

IT'S A CRUEL WORLD

It's no fun to be the kid everyone picks on. The developmental years of early puberty are the worst. Young teens can be relentlessly cruel to their peers with verbal and physical abuse. The effects of what happens during those school years can last a lifetime. Many adults admit their struggles with self-esteem and confidence come from the negative "tapes" they keep replaying in their minds—tapes that were permanently recorded in their memories when they were young teenagers.

Bullying has gotten a lot of attention since the tragic shootings at Columbine High School in 1999. Eric and Dylan, the two boys who brutally killed so many classmates, left angry written and videotaped messages, ranting about how they were going to repay their classmates for mistreating them. The bitterness and hurt building up inside them exploded with tragic results. Subsequent school shootings and the unparalleled cold-blooded violence at Virginia Tech often reveal the perpetrators of such horrific crimes as victims of bullying and social isolation.

Without question, shooting teachers and classmates is a sick and twisted response. But when you consider the verbal and social abuse some teens endure in school, it's not altogether surprising that deeply troubled young people might strike back in an effort to repay their abusers.

BULLYING: A SAFETY ISSUE?

The media pundits who express disbelief at teen violence just don't get it. "How can this happen?" they ask. If they look closely they'll see almost every school has abused and angry kids. These young people often feed their wounded spirits with violent games and images, imagining a day when they'll have the power to respond to the cruel people who bully them. When the next school shooting happens, the students you work with could be in the line of fire.

Your youth ministry has something vital and life changing to offer young people as they walk through the minefield of adolescent culture. Dr. James Dobson, founder of Focus on the Family, speaks about the importance of making your youth ministry a safe community—a place offering acceptance and true love to all young people regardless of the rejection they've experienced at school or in their families. In a hostile world a life-giving youth ministry has the opportunity to offer preemptive, pro-active safety to a community. Simple acceptance and respect opens the heart of a troubled young person to find genuine love in a community of peers. Schools become safer when protected by a growing force of young people who actively oppose bullying and stand up for peers when they are taunted and teased.

Youth ministry leaders have the opportunity and responsibility to fight the peer-to-peer verbal, physical, and sexual abuse so prevalent in our schools and youth culture. Our churches and communities cannot ignore or tolerate a bully culture. The safety of our young people demands we take stand.

WHAT IS BULLYING?

Bullying is any action by an individual or group that aims to physically or emotionally hurt another person on a regular basis. Bullying humiliates, belittles, and isolates people. Bullying behavior includes calling names, making threats, spreading rumors (verbally or on the Internet), taking or damaging a person's possessions, leaving people out, hitting, kicking, displaying racist attitudes, and sending nasty text messages.

When kids in your group are being bullied, you will see the results. They don't want to go to school or church; they lose their appetite; they become ill and frightened in social situations; they "lose" possessions and money; they withdraw from peers and family; they become aggressive and bully younger siblings; they may even attempt suicide.

Shortly after the Columbine shootings, Christian novelist Frank Peretti wrote *The Wounded Spirit* (also released with the alternate titles *No More Bullies* and *No More Victims*) where he revealed that bullies had abused him as a young teen. Peretti was born with a rare disfiguring health condition that affected his speech. When other kids made fun of him, he withdrew and retreated into a fantasy world of monsters and horror. These monsters—such as the Mummy, the Creature from the Black Lagoon, Frankenstein's monster, and others—were also misunderstood because of their physical characteristics. But they had power, and they used that power against their oppressors. In his escape world Frank felt important and powerful as he fantasized about hurting the kids who hurt him.

Peretti tells of how the pain and inner rage felt by someone mercilessly picked on can be released in unhealthy ways. When a young person is teased and tormented regularly, it leads to great hurt and bitterness that eventually comes out. Emotional wounds go very deep.

HOW BULLYING CAN INFILTRATE YOUTH MINISTRY

We give permission to bullies and enable them to abuse others when...

- We join in the laughter when weaker students are ridiculed.

- We do nothing to correct or stop verbal abuse.

- We let stronger kids use physical force on weaker kids.

- We tolerate and use negative and nasty nicknames given to kids.

- We make fun of kids according to their physical appearance.

- We stereotype certain groups of people as winners or losers.

- We plan only activities that require athletic skills.

- We give less attention to people who are not socially popular or attractive.

- We joke about overweight people (and serve only calorie-rich food at youth events).

- We show media images of only physically attractive people.

- We mimic the mistakes made by clumsy or socially awkward kids.

- We tell ourselves and others that being picked on is normal and should be ignored.

BUILDING A SAFE, BULLY-FREE ZONE

Most of us fall into one of three categories when it comes to bullying—bullies, victims, or bystanders. The goal is to break away from these categories and become an active protector of yourself and others.

Make bully-busting a topic of regular discussion in your youth meetings. Stress how important it is for the ministry to be a safe, bully-free space for all kids. Define clearly what behavior is unacceptable in your group and enforce that standard. Remind students that each of them is created and loved by God, and explain how that changes how we treat one another. Let kids know the youth group is a safe place where no bullying (not even a little bit) is permitted.

Show kids that your youth ministry is an open group where all people are welcome and accepted. Strive to make everyone feel valued and included. Diversify the activities of your youth ministry to make sure they connect with the interests of all your students, not just those who are the most athletic or popular. Develop and value the hidden talents and skills of all your kids, especially those who might get less affirmation and support in other social situations. Build the self-esteem of all your kids as they participate.

Confront the bullies in your group. Get under the tough guy/gal persona, and find out what drives them to hurt others. Help them feel loved, accepted, and powerful without expressing it through aggression. Praise their efforts to change and use their strength to protect others.

Teach kids to speak up and protect one another and the persecuted kids in their schools. Stress the difference between Christ's teaching and the normal attack-and-destroy world values. Help them understand and own the different value system your youth ministry practices. Challenge students to change their negative language toward others.

You can help change the rules about what is funny and who are winners and losers. If your students are using MySpace or similar networking Web sites, talk with them about writing positive, uplifting comments about people and shunning the gossip and hatred spewed out on targeted kids. Help them use their influence to speak up for what is right and protect the kids who are bullied.

We have the opportunity to help our students embrace their mission to befriend everyone at school—a mission that can transform their schools when put into practice. Make your youth ministry a safe place for young people who are hurting.

REFLECT AND INTERACT

Stop and reflect on your experiences and decisions related to the safety of young people. Better yet, discuss these questions with your youth ministry team:

- What personal history or experience have you had with bullying?

- Who attending your youth ministry meetings shows signs of being either a consistent bully or victim?

- To what bullying activity have you been merely a bystander? What action can you take?

- How safe and open is your youth ministry to kids who are different and out of the mainstream?

CAMPS, RETREATS, AND CONFERENCES

CHAPTER 9

I'll never forget my first day of church camp when I was in eighth grade. Mark, George, and I were the three musketeers, primed and ready to run wild and meet girls. By the end of that first day, the three of us had spent most of our time focused on the same female.

She was older and more mature than the other girls at camp. Mark met her during the softball game when a bat thrown 30 feet straight up came down squarely on the top of his head. George met her 30 minutes later, shortly after he crashed into the backstop chasing my errant throw from left field.

Not to be out done by my buddies, I met her that evening. I walked out of her cottage with a huge red mark on my neck. It wasn't from passion. I'd been running through the darkness between the buildings chasing girls when I was clotheslined by a metal stabilizing wire attached to a light pole. Our special lady took good care of us that first day, but we all agreed the camp nurse was a little too wrinkled for our eighth-grade tastes.

Crazy things always seemed to happen at camp. It was never like being home. New setting. New people. No parents. The counselors were young, fun loving, and sometimes wilder than the kids.

Thirteen years later I was a young youth pastor and the eighth-graders were chasing *me* through the darkness of an upstate New York camp. I had a piece of adhesive tape on my forehead, and they were determined to take it off. Our nighttime "wear 'em out" game was a creative adaptation of cops and robbers. The tape on my forehead meant I was still alive. When it was ripped off, I was "dead."

Apparently, my number was up. Three husky guys wrestled me to the ground and began pawing at my face. It stopped being fun when their fingernails ripped across my nose and eyes. At that moment I realized there were 800 fingers pawing at 160 eyes all across that camp. I thought I had created a wild and crazy camp game designed to let my junior high kids do what they did best—chase and tussle with one another. Instead I might easily have been the architect of serious injury or eye damage for one or more of them.

GOING CAMP CRAZY

Thinking back on my cops-and-robbers game, I realize the camp attitude had overridden my good sense. I doubt I would have run this game at a normal youth group activity back home. I wanted my kids to be excited about being at camp. There's nothing wrong with wanting students to have great memories of camp. But the camp atmosphere seems to encourage leaders to loosen the safety standards when, in fact, the situation calls for them to be strengthened.

Think about it. Do we let our young people run unchecked in the dark through the hallways of our church building or outside on church property at night? Yet many of us allow it when we are at an outdoor camp setting full of surprises and hazards.

Linda organized a late-night hide-and-seek game for her youth group at their fall retreat. During the game she got scared as she watched her crew run through the woods, jump off ledges, and crash into one another. One girl ran into a clothesline (sound familiar?) and ended up on the ground with the wind knocked out of her. When Linda tried to calm their reckless approach to the game, it suddenly wasn't much fun.

At breakfast the next morning, she saw one of her girls cradling her arm tenderly. An x-ray that afternoon showed a broken bone. The girl hadn't said anything about the injury the night before because she didn't want to spoil all the fun. During the drive home Linda mentally practiced how she was going to explain to the parents exactly what was going on when the accident occurred.

Camp is different. Things happen there that don't happen at home—adventure, romance, activities, spiritual openness, and accidents. The basic safety risk for camps and retreats is underestimating how different the camp setting is and the potential safety hazards involved. Too often we walk into the facility with a relaxed attitude toward safety.

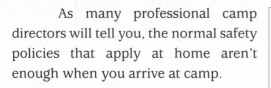
As many professional camp directors will tell you, the normal safety policies that apply at home aren't enough when you arrive at camp.

INGREDIENTS FOR SAFE CAMPS AND RETREATS

THE CAMP DIRECTOR

Safe and successful camps start with a relationship—youth leader and camp director working together. Some camp directors are actively involved in every aspect of the camp, while others focus on providing basic maintenance for the buildings and facilities. The youth leader should visit the camp and talk with the camp director months in advance in order to establish a positive and smooth working relationship.

> ### THE RULES OF EMERGENCY RESPONSE
> 1. Think before you act.
> 2. Get yourself and others away from immediate danger.
> 3. Take control of your group.
> 4. Calm emotions of people in your group.
> 5. Assess any injuries and treatment needed.
> 6. Think and talk together about what to do next.
> 7. Take action to get help without taking additional unnecessary risk.

We got off to a really bad start with a camp director in New England during a winter retreat. During our first 30 minutes on the grounds, students broke a light and a chair. The camp director got very gruff with us. During supper one of our staff flicked some chocolate pudding onto a student at the table, setting off a minor pudding war. The camp director rushed out of the dishwashing room, grabbed the microphone, and chewed out all our students and staff.

The camp director sensed we weren't going to control our students, so he stepped in to protect his property. I am embarrassed to confess we allowed our staff to make fun of "Mr. Grumpy" in all the meetings the rest of the weekend and joked with the teenagers about trashing the camp. (I found out later that several other church groups had caused significant damage at the camp in the weeks prior to our visit.)

Are youth leaders and camp directors partners or adversaries? Experienced camp directors feel pressure when hosting youth leaders who are soft on safety issues. Their sense of responsibility compels them to step in and speak up before someone is injured. Ideally they can use the moment to educate leaders to the risks and dangers they've learned from experience, but they know they risk becoming the bad guy. Pre-trip meetings in which activities and safety standards are discussed in detail can prevent misunderstanding and bad feelings.

Safe camps and retreats start with a partnership between host and visitor. Many camps offer the services of professional staff, such as lifeguards, watercraft instructors, or winter sports supervisors, to lead or supervise activities, as well as registered nurses or other staff with medical training. When preparing for a camp visit, find out the instruction and supervision the camp staff can provide your group. For an additional fee some camps will add additional, experienced staff to the team of workers serving and protecting your group.

THE CAMP FACILITIES

Nothing beats seeing a camp firsthand and meeting with the director. In addition to eyeballing the campground, inquire about the accreditation of the camp. The most reputable accreditation is with the American Camping Association (ACA), a secular organization with strict safety standards for physical buildings, staffing, programs, and services. Christian camps may also be associated with Christian Camping International (CCI), which requires a high standard of excellence. Investigating a camp's accreditation and association membership gives a strong basis for judging its quality.

Camps with ACA or CCI accreditation maintain high standards for facilities, staff, and program. If the camp or retreat house you're using isn't part of ACA or CCI, be certain to investigate these primary safety issues on site before using the facility:

- Check that the buildings and sleeping quarters are protected with working smoke detectors, recently serviced fire extinguishers, and emergency exits.

- Walk through the camp observing electrical wiring, sanitary conditions, storage of hazardous materials, and other potential dangers.

- Ask about the accident record at the camp during the past 12 months.

- Inspect the sports equipment and facilities of the camp to determine how well they are maintained.

- Learn of the accessibility of medical facilities and services.

- Ask what professional staff are available to you through the camp (registered nurses, lifeguards, waterfront instructors, etc.)

- Ask about the insurance coverage the camp carries that would apply to you and your group.

THE FOOD SERVICE

Whether you decide to use the camp's food service or provide your own cooks, you must give special attention to food preparation. Accidents on the waterfront or sledding hill are rare and usually affect only one person, but a lapse in safety standards in the kitchen could cause the whole group to suffer food poisoning. Again, if your selected camp location is not ACA or CCI certified, don't be afraid to ask these questions:

- Does the cook have training and experience in food service for large groups?

- Are the utensils, equipment, serving dishes, and food contact areas clean and sanitized?

- Is a dishwasher available to wash at legal standards of 100°F and rinse at 180°F? Are all items allowed to air dry?

- Are perishable foods refrigerated at temperatures below 45°F when they are not being served?

- Are precautions taken to prevent salmonella poisoning? (Salmonella bacteria are present in some uncooked eggs and some raw poultry.)

THROUGH THE EYES OF A CAMP DIRECTOR

What "safety sins" do camp directors see when the average youth group arrives for a week-end retreat?

- The type of drivers and condition of the vehicles are major reasons for concern.

- The program and activities have been planned with little regard for safety and little communication with the camp director.

- The church group is reluctant to spend a little extra money for additional services or added staff supervision for the activities.

- Groups who want to do their own food preparation underestimate the safety risks in the kitchen.

- Instead of planning the camp experience together and working to protect all the young people, the youth leader and camp director become adversaries when they disagree about safety issues.

- Are workers required to wash hands frequently?

- Is smoking prohibited in food preparation and service areas?

- Are sharp knives and slicing machines used only by adults?

- Can the menu be adjusted if people in your group have severe peanut, milk, or gluten allergies?

STAFF TRAINING AND EMERGENCY PREPAREDNESS

Here's a pop quiz for you and your camp counselors: *What's the first rule of emergency response?* You can't prepare your leaders for every bad possibility, but they need to know the basics so they can respond effectively to the unexpected.

It was a stormy night. The camp counselors and girls in one cabin were jolted out of their sleep by a loud crash on the roof. The girls in the cabin began screaming and crying. Wind and rain were pounding against the cabin. It was totally dark; apparently, the electrical power had been knocked out. What should the counselors do?

Thankfully these counselors kept the first rule of emergency response in mind.

The first rule of emergency response is to think before you act. The counselors quieted the girls and did a quick roll call to make sure no one had been injured. With everyone okay they gathered the girls together and calmed them. They took control of the group and their emotions.

Calmly they talked about what they should do. Because they were safe and not being threatened by any conditions, they decided to stay put until help came or daylight allowed them to see and better assess the situation. That was a life-saving decision, because electrical power lines had fallen onto the porch of their cabin. Anyone stepping out of the cabin in the dark would probably have been electrocuted.

When the storm hit, a member of the camp staff who was assigned to emergency response got up to inspect the camp. He saw the electrical lines down on the cabin porch and returned to the camp's electrical box to shut down the power. He'd never before shut down the power for the camp in that manner, but there was an emergency response notebook available to him that described what he should do.

The counselors' response was the product of "what if" training. They hadn't specifically discussed the possibility of a tree falling on the cabin, but they knew they should think before taking any action. They made sure everyone was safe and then proceeded slowly and cautiously. If anyone had panicked and run out the front door, this would have brought tragedy.

"There is no substitute for trained, mature staff," says Bob Kobielush, president of Christian Camping International. Weekend counselors from our local youth groups need basic "what if" training. Such training should include the following:

- Do they know where the emergency exits are in case of a fire?

- Do they have the number of the police or ambulance crew?

- Do they have access to a telephone?

- Do they have an emergency phone number for a camp staff person who is available 24 hours a day?

- Do they know to whom they should report any trouble? How can that person be reached?

- Do they know where to find a first aid kit?

Give counselors as much information and training as possible. Talk through a wide variety of possible emergencies until the basics of immediate response are ingrained in your leaders.

All staff members and leaders need a briefing on emergency procedures prior to the camp or retreat. Rehearse basic safety procedures and response. The leader can select possible events and quiz each staff member on how to respond. Written instructions and information on securing medical help should be provided.

REDUCING INJURIES: OUTDOOR CAMP GAMES

Here are some guidelines for safer outdoor games:

- Don't play on any athletic field without first inspecting it for hazards, such as holes and dangerous debris.

- Don't use games that encourage any throwing of objects toward another person's face.

- Don't mix big and small, weak and strong students in contact sports. The smaller kids usually get crunched.

- Don't make everyone in your group play the sports game. The reluctant participant is often the first one injured.

- Don't encourage aggressive or rough play.

- Don't let athletic equipment be used without supervision.

- Don't hesitate to step in and stop a situation that is getting too rowdy, rough, or out of control.

I once helped create a sports situation that almost turned into a very ugly scene. At a summer youth conference, groups were encouraged to enter athletic teams in various sports for competition during the week. The boys basketball division was really lopsided. Most teams were weak and unskilled, but there were two teams loaded with varsity athletes.

Instead of running the tournament as usual, I joined other leaders in suggesting the two top teams play a best-of-five series for the championship. What seemed like a great idea on Monday had us practically calling the National Guard on Friday. We had encouraged competition between these two teams from different cities and backgrounds. Every day the games got more

PARLEZ VOUS FRANCAIS?

"Non parle francais," I repeated into the phone. "I need to speak to someone who speaks English." I was very frustrated. This was the fourth hospital I'd called trying to find a girl from my youth group. How many hospitals are in Montreal anyway?

Our holiday conference in downtown Montreal had given students the option of snow sledding at Mount Royal Park. One student came rushing back to the hotel to tell me her friend Liz had crashed into a group of guys at the bottom of the hill. Her nose met someone's knee, and an ambulance had come and taken her to a hospital. The medical team spoke French. The student had no idea what they said.

It had taken the student an hour to find me at the hotel. My calls to different hospitals had taken another hour. We finally found Liz in the sixth hospital. I got directions and caught a cab (we had come on coach buses) to the hospital. She'd been sitting there untreated for almost three hours. When I arrived with the permission slip, we called her parents and decided that any plastic surgery on her broken nose would be done at home in New York. Later that night I put her on a plane home.

Our safety and supervision plan was weak at best. We had staff at the park, but no one had a list of all the students or permission slips for them. One member of our staff had seen the ambulance and crowd from a distance but didn't know one of "our kids" was involved. Liz sat alone in the hospital in pain, untreated for three hours because I had not planned ahead for her safety.

intense. The level of the players was far above the skill of the referees to control the game and make the calls. When the final gun sounded in game five, players and their fans were ready to fight. It took a long time to cool the players down. We'd encouraged too much competition and allowed it to get out of control.

Good supervision of sports activities means watching for when participants are growing angry and looking to get revenge for what's been done to them. Be assertive and pull these students out of the game until they cool down. The gung-ho kid who's swinging crazily in the giant pillow fight needs to feel a staff member's hand on his shoulder, cautioning him to ease up or sit out.

A group of churches in Florida sponsored a big day of field events. It almost became a tragedy during the first hour when a young man had a severe asthma attack. The staff admitted later that they weren't sure what to do to help that young man. The tragedy was avoided because the local church network leader had secured two paramedics from a nearby Navy base to be at the event. They moved in with their equipment and restored the young man's regular breathing.

Whenever I walk into a camp director's office at the start of multi-day camp, I look at my phone and pray I won't have to use it to call some mom or dad with bad news. With good safety preparation and enforcement, your camps and retreats can be positive lifetime memories for your students.

HOTELS AND RESORTS

Increasingly youth groups are attending large conferences held at hotels and resorts. The rustic, remote campground has been replaced by the Marriott or the Radisson. While there's room for debate about the merits of using a hotel over a camp, the hotel definitely raises some unique safety issues.

Most hotels are multi-story buildings in highly populated areas. If the design of the hotel includes balconies and high overlooks, be prepared to have some young person dangerously leaning over the railing or sitting on it like a bird on a perch. If the windows can open, kids will be tempted to hang out of them or throw objects to the ground. Strict warnings and attentive staff supervision are absolutely necessary.

Swimming pools, hot tubs, and saunas are an attractive part of the hotel experience. The swimming pools tend to be small and overcrowded during a youth conference. Be sure to have a hotel employee or a qualified conference staff member serving as lifeguard and enforcing safety standards. Make sure that students follow the written safety rules posted near the sauna and hot tubs and that the hot tubs are cleaned and maintained throughout the weekend. A build up of bacteria in the water can cause illness to all bathers. If a hotel is not usually busy on weekends, its normal maintenance schedule may not be adequate for your weekend invasion.

Although hotel accommodations are usually much nicer than a camp setting, the small rooms jammed with teenagers (usually four per room with two double beds) and the locked doors present supervision problems. Students have much more privacy. It is harder for staff to just "walk in" and discover some inappropriate behavior. Guys and girls have more opportunity for a romantic rendezvous undetected by staff. Instruction and enforcement of rules prohibiting coed gatherings in bedrooms is absolutely necessary. Set up designated public areas in the hotel for coed hangout spots. Staff must be diligent about guy-girl encounters in the private rooms.

The privacy of the rooms and the access to public shopping areas also increase the possibility of contraband materials (alcohol, drugs, etc.) being present at the conference. Students who are looking for trouble have an uncanny knack of finding the wrong people. Rules need to be clear and tough. Staff must be polite but tenacious about such destructive substances.

A clear policy about leaving the hotel property must be communicated to all students and staff. If a shopping or amusement area is nearby, under what circumstances can your young people take advantage of it? No one should be walking or sightseeing alone. Staff supervisors should either be with every group of young people or should know where they will be and when they will return. The type of staff supervision needed may vary according to the setting or the reputation of the area, but staff members need to know the rules and enforce them strictly.

Using a hotel or resort site shifts your retreat from a remote, protected location to a public site. The normal operations of the hotel and the area will continue throughout your conference experience, allowing your young people contact with all sorts of people. The leader needs to prepare for strangers who could harm the young people. These "strangers" may even be on the hotel or resort staff.

Our group was staying at a hotel in Florida for a winter-break conference. A 16-year-old girl asked to be excused from an evening meeting to return to her room for some headache medicine. We had a staff person watch her walk across the courtyard to her room. When she arrived at her room, she turned to see three men 25-to-30-years-old following close behind her. They had just come from the hotel bar and were looking for some action. They tried to talk her into inviting them into her room. When she refused, one man grabbed her and pushed himself up against her. She screamed and the staff leader on watch outside the meeting room came running. The police were called, and they escorted the men off the property and warned them not to return. The young woman felt fear and anxiety throughout the rest of the week.

At another winter conference in a downtown hotel, a middle-aged man stepped onto an elevator filled with 14-year-old girls. As the elevator moved from floor to floor, he tried to start conversations with some of the girls. They did their best to ignore him and exited at their floor. One girl was left in the elevator alone with this man. The doors closed before she realized her dangerous situation. The man approached her and began to touch her inappropriately. When the door opened she jumped out and ran for her room. Her youth leader met her in the hall, and they began searching for hotel security guards. In the process they spotted the offender heading for the main door of the hotel. They followed in hot pursuit, finally finding a security guard near the door as the offender was disappearing into the parking lot. Security guards searched the parking areas and issued a warning and a description to all hotel personnel.

In both instances the parents of the girls were called immediately and informed of the situation. They were given full information and consulted about what they wanted done. The girls were given counseling and special staff escort until they felt more relaxed and secure.

Other strangers are less hostile but still dangerous. The young men of the towns we visit always seem to find our group and our girls. Some of it is innocent—a casual conversation on the beach or in a store brings them to visit our girls in the evening. Usually they arrive with a couple male buddies to check us out. We are very up-front with our visitors. They are welcomed into the meeting or activities. We keep staff eyes on them throughout their visit. We tell them the ground rules the girls must follow, including the regulation that no one from our group is allowed to leave the grounds with them.

Our students get similar straightforward reminders from staff about leaving the hotel, keeping the rules, and continuing to be involved in the required activities. We try to keep our conversations with visitors upbeat and positive. These encounters provide great opportunities for staff to talk about the purpose of the group and our faith in Jesus Christ. Sometimes it generates genuine interest. Others are driven away by it. (Apparently sharing your faith in Jesus can also be effective as a security technique.)

At no time should any student ever get into a vehicle with someone he or she just met. The risk of an attack on our young people by a stranger should never be underestimated.

STAFFING AND SUPERVISION
SMALLER RATIO NEEDED

It is worth the extra cost to provide one staff leader for every three or four students at a hotel/resort setting. You can negotiate with most hotels to allow one adult in every room with four students by using a rollaway bed or putting a sleeping bag on the floor. With some students you may want to lock the windows and put the staff member on the floor in front of the door at night. The ratio could be one-to-seven if the hotel provides adjoining rooms (and the door is left open) or if trusted student leaders are assigned to the room. When two or more junior high students are assigned to a room, an adult should always be rooming with them.

WATCHING OVER THE FLOCK

Imagine a friend has arranged for your church youth group to spend the weekend at a church on the edge of a major city. Your plan is to take the youth downtown to see the tourist sights.

- What safety precautions must you take to be sure everyone has a great time and returns home safely?
- If you are going to use mass transit, how will you keep everyone together?
- How will you respond when members of your group want to stop and look at attractions not on your plan?
- Will you allow students to go off in pairs or groups to window shop on their own?
- What instructions will you give to students about dealing with people who might approach them?
- What will you do if someone is missing when you are ready to leave?

These "field trip" experiences are best supervised by breaking the large group into smaller groups, each chaperoned by an adult leader who has been briefed thoroughly concerning the details of the trip and safety concerns. Allowing students to wander unsupervised in an unfamiliar city or resort area has grown increasingly dangerous.

SLEEPING ARRANGEMENTS

With the heightened sensitivity to sexual abuse and allegations of sexual abuse, it is no longer recommended to have an adult sleeping in the same bed with a student. Often the adult can sleep on a rollaway bed or a sleeping bag on the floor as an alternative. Some groups assign only two students and one adult per room and have the adult sleep alone in one of the double beds.

Some students or parents may have particular concerns around sleeping arrangements if you have teens who are openly gay or lesbian in your group. It's essential to have a clear standard of relational and sexual conduct that applies to *all* students. Communicate that standard and enforce it equally. When possible, it's best if every student has his or her own bed (or sleeping bag), to reduce the possibility of sexual contact.

Leaders should encourage students to disrobe or change clothing privately in the bathroom. The leader should do so as well.

ROOM SAFETY ORIENTATION

Remember the little diagram on the inside of every hotel door? Be sure to look it over with your students so they all know the closest exit and the importance of using the stairs and not the elevators in an emergency. It might be their first time staying above the first floor in a hotel.

STAFF-STUDENT ASSIGNMENTS

Have each staff member supervise the students they room with throughout the trip. Each staff person should check the attendance of his or her students at every meeting and meal. If anyone is not present, the staff person needs to take action to find the missing student and get him or her there. The same is true for activities and curfew. Throughout the conference staff members should spend their time mixing normally and naturally with their students and sharing activities with them (not the other adults). This not only provides opportunities for relational evangelism and discipleship, but it also puts adults in situations where safety can be enforced quietly and effectively.

SECURITY

Staff and volunteers need written instructions about whom to call (with phone numbers) in case of emergency situations. A staff supervisor should check every room shortly after curfew to verify all students are in their assigned rooms. If anyone is missing the supervising staff should follow a preplanned course of action. During the day every student should be accounted for and under someone's supervision. On our weeklong trips to Florida, some students ask to stay at the hotel during the day rather than go to the beach. In those cases we assign staff members to stay with the students and give them a written list with the students' names and room numbers. They stay in contact with those students during the day.

STAFF TEAM SPIRIT

Although each staff member is assigned to a particular group of students, all staff must be willing to approach any student who needs supervision. When a student is standing on a balcony ledge or throwing ice in the hall, the adult leader should step in even if he or she does not know the particular young person. Any correction should be done respectfully and privately. No yelling or sarcasm is necessary. Young people will respect adults who approach them personally (My name is _____, what's yours?) and rationally (We don't want you doing that because...).

STAYING IN TOUCH

If your group is at a large conference where students have many options for eating and entertainment, set up a group check-in time once or twice each day during which every student and staff member reports to a leader either individually or as a group. You don't want to go through the whole day without seeing your students or knowing where they're going. Regular contact usually means fewer surprises and problems.

STAFF COMMUNICATION

Staff communication is key to having a conference experience that is both fun and safe. Prepare your volunteers for their assignments. Let them know what decisions they are responsible for, what decisions will come from you (the leader), and how your decisions will be communicated to them.

REFLECT AND INTERACT

Stop and reflect on your experiences and decisions related to the safety of young people. Better yet, discuss these questions with your youth ministry team:

- What accidents and injuries do you see most often at a camp or retreat setting? What have you done to reduce the injuries?

- How can the risk of sexual abuse by adults or peer-to-peer sexual activity be reduced at a camp or retreat setting?

- What's the best camp game you know that is both fun and safe?

- What additional preparations can you take to ensure that your next camp or conference is better and safer for your students?

MISSION TRIPS: HOME AND ABROAD

CHAPTER 10

Youth leaders are introducing today's young people to the world. The kids come home exhausted and penniless because they've given everything they had to help the people they went to serve—and paid to do it. And those kids can't wait to go back.

What a remarkable generation of young people we serve. They want their youth ministry experience to be much more than fun and games. Mission trips and work camps continue to grow in size and impact because they help students move their faith from head knowledge to hands-on application.

Problems are problems wherever you go—but the farther you travel away from home, the more serious and complicated problems can become. Taking young people to work in mission settings within the United States or internationally generates special safety issues.

WHO'S YOUR PARTNER?

International mission trips and domestic work camps require serious partnership. This process begins at home. The local church or youth organization needs a seasoned leader with travel and work experience. Don't put a rookie in charge when the project involves taking kids far from home. For the best results and most meaningful work projects, partner with a reputable mission organization with a strong track record. Link your efforts to their leadership. Let the experienced professionals do the set-up work.

Getting started with a mission organization might require a pre-trip inspection to determine how the group operates in the location you plan to visit. You want an organization that can deliver what it promises and that has the resources and contacts to resolve problems. In the early stages of planning an international trip, check the U.S. government's Web site on foreign travel to look for any warnings or cautions about your destination country. Keep checking the site as your departure date gets closer. If warnings indicate increased trouble, you would be wise to postpone the trip. Think like a parent.

If your group will be traveling to a non-English speaking location, insist that your host provide reliable translators to travel with you. The quality of the mission organization and the local host you work with is the most influential factor in how your group responds to the trip.

PREPARING THE STUDENTS

Student preparation should include applications and release and health forms signed by parents. If the project is outside the United States or Canada, requirements may include health exams and shots. Passports are now required for travel to and from Canada, Mexico, and the Caribbean, where not too long ago just a driver's license would do. Tell the group to expect delays when applying for new or renewed passports and to avoid trying to get one at the last minute. Double the amount of time the passport office says it will need to complete the processing.

Church youth leaders with successful mission trips prequalify their student participants. They require orientation, training meetings, and study programs several months in advance. You want your students to be committed and confident about being on this mission trip.

Youth leaders can also provide pre-trip practical training to get the maximum amount accomplished. If your group is doing a work project that involves building, repairing, or doing construction, students should be oriented and trained on local pre-trip projects in order to learn basic skills. Don't assume your kids will know how to work or have any construction skills. Teach them how to use tools properly, how to lift heavy objects, and how to safely use a ladder. Ladders and roofs are involved in many accidents each year.

If students will be doing carpentry work or painting, take time to train them in those skills prior to the trip. Many groups limit the use of power tools to adults. No one should use power tools without proper safety training. The use of power tools should always require

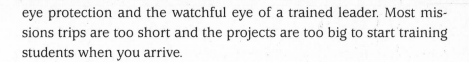

eye protection and the watchful eye of a trained leader. Most missions trips are too short and the projects are too big to start training students when you arrive.

KEEPING PARENTS INFORMED AND INVOLVED

Parents need clear, specific information about the logistics of the whole trip. Be sure to talk with them about the work their young people will do on the project. Remember, parents need complete travel information as well as prior knowledge of any activities involving power tools. You win the confidence of the parents with frequent communication and thorough information. Your credibility with parents will have a lot to do with how you operate the youth program week to week at home. They see your problem-solving and organizational skills 50 weeks during the year. The way you operate at home indicates how you'll operate in another state or country with added pressure on you.

The information about what your group will be doing should be written on the consent form parents sign. Parents don't like to be surprised. After one church's trip students came home with tales of how they'd repaired the roofs of houses in a poor neighborhood. Parents complained that their young people had no experience doing that kind of work and should not have been on the roofs without safety training. The kids had a great time, but the parents were probably right.

Parents want to see emergency phone numbers and a plan for how you will communicate with them at home while you are traveling and at the worksite. Web sites and e-mail give you opportunities to send regular communications and photos to the folks at home. Whatever communication you agree to do, be sure to do it. Don't leave parents anxious and angry because the promised communication never came.

WORK TEAMS

You should have at least two leaders on even the smallest work trip (in case of illness or injury), and the leaders should match the gender make-up of the student team. You should have at least one adult to every four to six students, depending on the project and setting. Use this ratio as the basis for work teams and small breakout groups during the trip. While traveling the large group should move as a series of small groups—with each leader keeping track of his or her students and getting them to the right place at the right time. Linking each leader to a small group also ensures that leaders hear the problems and concerns of the students every day and can inform the overall team leader if action is needed to resolve the problems.

AIR AND GROUND TRAVEL

Traveling as a group is a big part of the whole experience. Make your travel plans carefully, and expect them to change. You'll need to be flexible and positive to reduce the stress on any young people traveling for the first time and all the parents waiting nervously at home. Give your group clear instructions before you start your trip. Help them understand what to expect as they pass through airport security or ride many hours in the van. Head counts are essential to make sure everyone is with you. Don't lose anyone in the airport or leave anyone at a rest stop on the highway. Take time to double check before leaving a stop. Be sure your adult leaders are keeping track of their assigned students.

Ground transportation is a key challenge on any trip. Bringing your own vehicle is most reliable. Be sure everyone uses a seatbelt at all times—no exceptions. Be sure all luggage and equipment is packed safely and securely. Make a plan to stop regularly at rest stops or shopping areas so students can get out and move around.

When flying to a distant location and renting a van or being transported by the host organization, follow the same safety rules. Work with the local host to ensure your group is safe when you travel in the country. Driving in another country can be different and quite dangerous. It's best to have a local driver. You may find that seatbelt rules and vehicle capacity guidelines are ignored in some foreign situations. This may force the group leader to make some difficult decisions that are respectful of the local culture while, at the same time, protecting the work team. These decisions are best handled months in advance by asking specific questions about ground transportation and stating clearly what safety standards need to be met for your group to make the trip.

HEALTH

Work teams must take special precautions to stay healthy at work sites nationally and internationally. Here are some health-related lessons groups have learned during their travels.

1. Be sure every member of your group brings plenty of heavy-duty sunscreen, a hat, and sunglasses. Apply the sunscreen generously and often. Sunburn is the most frequent injury. Severe sunburn can incapacitate a team member for several days. Do not work without a shirt or in a skimpy top; the purpose of the trip is to help others, not to sunbathe. Any trip that takes you farther south or to a higher altitude than where you live exposes your group to more intense sun than you normally experience.

2. Drink plenty of fluids, especially when working in hot, humid conditions. Find a good source of reliable water for your group. Even within the USA the water in some rural and urban areas can taste much different from what you are used to at home. Bring bottled water with your group, and look for local outlets where you can buy cases of bottled water.

On overseas mission trips, finding good water may be difficult. This is where working with a good sponsoring group can make it easier to find what your group needs. When you are in a country with bad water quality, remember that tap water shouldn't be used for brushing your teeth or as ice in your drinks.

When working in a hot, humid climate, the challenge is to stay hydrated. Dehydration poses a serious health risk. Without adequate hydration students will be unable to work and will become ill. A good guide to determine proper hydration is the ability to urinate at least once every two hours while working or exercising. If you cannot, you're not drinking enough fluids. Sometimes students refuse to drink liquids during the first few days of a mission trip because they don't want to use the primitive bathroom facilities. That's a big mistake. Leaders need to make sure their students are drinking enough water.

3. In foreign countries do not go swimming in fresh water before consulting with your missionary host about the dangers. The lakes and ponds in some areas of the world have parasites that can enter the body through the skin.

4. Do not walk around in bare feet unless you are swimming or at the beach. Protect your feet. Boots should be worn at all times in work areas. Give special attention to lacing and tying your boots. If you are asked to dig in the dirt with your hands, wear gloves. Hookworm (a type of parasite) enters the body through the skin. Dirt under your fingernails can also contain parasite eggs that may get into your mouth and enter your system. Dress like workers, not like tourists or sunbathers. Be sensitive to the customs and dress standards of the country where you are working. In many countries, showing a lot of skin is not acceptable, especially for women.

5. In foreign countries do not eat any fruits or vegetables that you cannot boil or peel (such as bananas and oranges). Do not eat any fruit without washing and peeling it.

6. Expect to get diarrhea. Even the slight changes in traveling to other parts of the United States or Canada can cause intestinal disturbances. Control diarrhea with over-the-counter medicines, such as, Kaopectate or prescription drugs, such as, Parapectolin or Lomotil.

7. Every team member needs to get an updated tetanus shot. Other shots may be required for entrance to certain foreign countries to prevent typhoid, typhus, cholera, yellow fever, and hepatitis. Anti-malaria pills may also be required.

8. If you have allergies or other medical conditions, bring the medication you will need. Leaders need to be fully aware of every student's medical information. Students should not be taking medication without the leader's knowledge and permission. Some groups have run into problems when students seek to self-medicate and take too many pain-relief pills, such as, Tylenol with codeine. No medication should be brought on the trip from home without the leader's and parent's knowledge.

9. Be careful in tropical environments. Never antagonize animals or insects that could harm you. Tarantulas and scorpions are rarely deadly, but they can cause serious injury. Black widow spiders, fire ants, and killer bees are very dangerous. Treat them with respect.

10. Immediately treat any broken skin or laceration. Infection spreads much more quickly in tropical environments.

11. When eating native meals in another country, eat light to moderate amounts. Don't eat excessive amounts of foods that are unfamiliar to you.

12. Many travelers eat yogurt with an active culture every day for two weeks prior to an overseas trip. This may help prepare your digestive tract for the different foods you'll eat during the trip. You can also take acidophilus pills for the same benefit.

13. If anyone becomes sick, separate the person from the group for at least 24 hours. Place him or her in a special "sick" room. Only the staff leader should be allowed to visit the sick individual and bring food, medicine, and other supplies. If the person is truly sick, the isolation will protect the team and provide the sick person with privacy and quiet for sleep. If the person is just complaining to get out of work, 24 hours in isolation will change his or her mind and will discourage whining and complaining.

ACCIDENTS

Anticipate possible accidents, and seek to prevent them before they happen. Young people will take chances. They often will not think ahead or look for danger. Lacking experience, they put themselves in dangerous situations. The leader must be there to correct and protect them.

When a young person is injured or becomes ill, the leader is wise to make the maximum effort in seeking treatment. On a trip to the Caribbean, a young lady complained of stomach pains. A trip to the hospital brought a diagnosis of appendicitis. The leader spent much time on the phone with the parents back home, sharing all information so they could make an informed decision. The group had a nurse with them (always a smart idea) who helped interpret what the doctors were recommending. The young girl was flown back to the United States for additional examination before proceeding with the operation. That was what the parents wanted. The group leader handled the crisis intelligently and carefully.

A young man was struck in the eye with a piece of sheet metal during a hurricane clean-up trip to Florida. The staff took him to the hospital for immediate help and continued to check on him every couple of hours after returning to the camp. The student told the staff everything was fine. At the same time he was telling his mother a different story about the condition of his eye. When the alarmed mother contacted the staff and demanded action, the staff leaders did not respond defensively or in anger. They did what the mother 600 miles away wanted done and had a more honest talk with the student about the condition of his eye. Smart move.

What trips are you planning for your youth group this year? Regardless of your destination or the amount of comfort your accommodations will provide, the keys to a safe trip are advance planning, effective training of staff, and immediate response by the leader to problems. Be diligent and spend significant time discussing and preparing for safety concerns. The motto of experienced camp leaders stresses the importance of thorough preparation: "You get what you inspect, not what you expect."

REFLECT AND INTERACT

Stop and reflect on your experiences and decisions related to the safety of young people. Better yet, discuss these questions with your youth ministry team:

- How can a specialized mission organization help you plan and experience a successful missions trip? What can they do that you are not able to do?

- What preparations are needed to give parents confidence when their children travel to a foreign country?

- What is a safe ratio of adult staff to students on an international mission trip?

SUMMER SPORTS

All week we'd been playing those Beach Boys surfing songs real loud at our winter camp meetings on the east coast of Florida. Unfortunately the water had been absolutely flat for three days. The surfboards and boogie boards we'd brought from New York had not caught a single wave.

On the last day of our trip, the wind shifted and blew in a storm off the ocean. While most students sought shelter from the rain and wind, our surfer wannabes ran right past the lifeguard and straight into the ocean now churning with four-to-six-foot waves.

Within minutes our guys and gals were getting tossed in every direction by the waves. They ignored the lifeguard's whistle signaling them to get out of the water. Our staff had a strange mixture of reactions. Yes, it seemed a little dangerous, but this *was* their last day to have the kind of ocean fun we'd promised them. If they were crazy enough to be in the water in the middle of this storm, how could we stop them?

When the storm subsided, we'd not lost anyone. Several guys had raspberry scrapes on their backs and shoulders from being slammed into the sand by powerful waves. Others told about how scared they'd been when the waves were tossing them around like clothes in a dryer. On that day we stood silently and watched our students surf through the storm. Should we have stepped in and ordered them out of the water?

WATER SAFETY

Is water recreation a real danger or just a perceived risk? According to the National Safety Council, about 6,000 Americans drown every year. Only motor vehicle accidents and falls cause more accidental deaths. Drowning is the result of boating accidents, swimming activities, and accidental falls into water. In wilderness settings 85 percent of fatal accidents involve water.

Some of us feel relaxed around water and are comfortable including various types of water recreation activities in our youth ministry. Others see water as a dangerous element of God's creation and give it the utmost respect. This chapter surveys several popular water recreation activities and raises safety concerns related to youth ministry.

WATER-SAFETY STANDARDS

The American Camping Association (ACA) requires camps offering aquatic programs to meet strict standards of certification for their water-safety staff. How do the water recreation events in your ministry measure up to these standards?

WHO IS THE LIFEGUARD?

Are you protected by one or more lifeguards who are trained and certified by a recognized group such as the American Red Cross, YMCA, U.S. Lifesaving Association, BSA Lifeguard, or Royal Lifesaving? Have the lifeguards demonstrated skill in rescue and emergency procedures specific to their situations? Are they trained and supervised to enforce established safety regulations, to provide necessary instruction, and to identify and manage environmental and other hazards related to the activity?

WHO HAS EMERGENCY RESPONSE SKILLS?

Is a staff person present and accessible who is certified in both American Red Cross Standard First Aid (or its equivalent) and cardiopulmonary resuscitation (CPR) as certified by the American Red Cross, American Heart Association, or their equivalent?

WHAT PREPARATIONS HAVE YOU MADE?

- Have you listed specific safety rules for water-related activity? Do you orient all the students to the safety rules and procedures prior to the activity?

- Do you have written procedures for emergency and accident responses? Are these procedures rehearsed periodically?

- Are students tested for swimming ability before they're allowed to participate in aquatic activities?

- Do the lifeguards and lookouts have a system that enables them to quickly account for all participants?

- Is rescue equipment readily available and in good repair?

The American Red Cross, YMCA, YWCA, and other organizations offer water-safety courses and comprehensive training for individuals. Textbooks and practical instruction will give leaders confidence in handling safety procedures and emergency responses around water activities.

The best water-safety preparation we can make is to have our youth swim under the supervision of a certified lifeguard. As adult leaders we must defer to the judgment and leadership of the lifeguard in matters of water safety and support him or her before our students. When we operate without a certified lifeguard, we take the heavy responsibility of safety upon ourselves. In either situation the general safety rules of swimming safety apply.

> The CD contains a number of printable handouts that you and your ministry leaders can use to help your ministry engage in water-related fun more safely.

SAFETY TIPS FOR SWIMMING

- Never allow swimming unattended by a lifeguard or trained adult.

- Know your swimming abilities. Don't test yourself or others in situations beyond your skills.

- Never swim alone. Use a buddy system.

- Never swim close to any areas designated for jet skis, sailboats, or motorboats.

- Never dive unless you're sure the water is sufficiently deep and the bottom is free of hazardous objects.

- Don't use flotation devices or water toys that might allow you to be carried far out into deep water.

- After sunset swim only in well-lighted areas.

- At the first flash of lightning, exit the water immediately.

- Follow instructions from lifeguards. Respect their decisions. Never fake an emergency.

At Lakes and Ponds

- Check the bottom for hazardous debris.

- Have a designated swimming area.

- Beware of pushing or fighting on rafts.

- Know where to get emergency assistance.

At the Ocean

- Swim near the lifeguard stand.

- Stay away from piers and pilings.

- Look out for dangerous aquatic life (jellyfish, stinging coral, etc.)

- Never try to swim against a strong ocean current. Drift with it, and swim diagonally across it.

- When caught in an undertow (shorter and deeper than a current), turn and go with it until you can swim a diagonal course to the shore.

- Follow the instructions of the lifeguards regarding surf conditions.

If you have students in your youth ministry who cannot swim, teach them. That would be a lifelong gift to them. Make a goal to have every student in your group become a competent swimmer. In addition encourage some of your student leaders to take lifeguard training offered by the Red Cross or YMCA. These organizations could provide your group top quality safety coverage while developing their life skills.

USING PRIVATE AND PUBLIC POOLS

Public pools with certified lifeguards on duty make your safety job much easier. Private pools put the safety responsibility back into your hands.

- Never allow swimming unattended by a trained adult.

- Forbid running, pushing, and fighting around the pool.

- Beware of the diving board. Use it cautiously.

- Don't overload the pool.

- Don't allow students to jump on top of one another.

- Forbid chicken fighting (riding on a person's shoulders).

- Don't allow anyone to be held underwater.

- Keep electrical devices away from the pool. Make sure electrical outlets are equipped with ground-fault switches.

- Keep emergency response equipment and phone numbers accessible.

Special note: In public pools be alert for possible sexual predators. Encourage your youth to dress modestly and to undress and shower privately and quickly in changing rooms. Supervise the dressing rooms appropriately, and report any suspicious actions by strangers.

Be alert for any adults or teens who might try to touch your students. A public pool is not the place for an adult leader to take a nap in the sun.

CANOEING / RAFTING / TUBING

For the best results and the safest conditions when canoeing, rafting, or tubing, you should find a reputable outfitter and arrange for the equipment, training, and supervision you need. The conditions can vary widely from flat, slow-moving water to fast-flowing rocky rapids. Obviously the deeper and faster the water, the greater the risk.

CANOEING SAFETY CHECKLIST

- Wear personal flotation devices (life jackets) in swift or rough water. Cushions are not reliable. Personal flotation devices should be U.S. Coast Guard approved and should be the proper type, size, and fit for each user.

- Flotation devices must be worn snug and tight. Loose life jackets are dangerous because they can hold a person underwater.

- Make sure everyone riding in the canoes can swim.

- Notify several people or officials about your trip route and estimated return.

- Stick to the planned route. If you depart from the anticipated path, rescuers or other people may have difficulty finding you in case of trouble or emergency.

- In wilderness country, don't be caught without a map or magnetic compass. Islands and lakes look alike. Portage trails seem to disappear if you don't watch the signs carefully.

- Never run a stretch of rapids or white water without knowing exactly what lies ahead. Before you attempt to run the river, walk along the fast stretch to check the conditions. If you have any doubt that you can make it safely, portage the canoes.

- Get off the water at the first warning of high winds or a storm.

- Never stand up in a canoe. It is safer to change places by going ashore to do so.

- Carry a properly stocked first aid kit, and know how to use it.

- Be sure your canoe is in proper balance. Don't overload it. The middle section of the canoe should be at least six inches above the water line.

- Always keep a bailing can and a large sponge aboard to remove the excess water on the bottom of the canoe.

- If you are caught in a squall, sit in the bottom of the canoe; if conditions warrant it, lie flat on the bottom in such a position that you can bail.

- If the canoe capsizes, hold on to the canoe and kick-swim it to shore. Canoes are buoyant and will float. Staying with the craft is safer than attempting to swim ashore.

- Learn how to right an upset canoe in the water. Learn how to reenter a swamped canoe.

- At the first sign of lightning, get out of the water and away from your metal canoe. Wait out the storm in a nearby shelter or under small trees.

- Avoid swinging the canoe paddles to splash another canoe.

- Avoid paddling a long straight course across a lake because storms can blow up quickly. Stay close to shore.

- Have a staff member present who holds the following certifications: American Red Cross Standard First Aid or the equivalent and cardiopulmonary resuscitation for the age level served from the American Red Cross, The American Heart Association, or the equivalent.

IN A DEEP, FAST RIVER

When canoeing in white water, a few additional safety precautions should be taken:

- In white water all canoeists should wear helmets to protect their heads from rocks and debris if their craft should capsize.

- Persons in rapidly flowing water should never be downstream from their canoe, since the water may push the canoe toward them with tremendous force and could cause great injury.

- Take great caution when trees and branches are down in the river. Canoeists in and out of their canoes can be pushed into these obstructions by the force of the river and held there, causing hypothermia or drowning.

STAFF SUPERVISION OF A CANOE TRIP

The maximum size for a controlled canoe trip is eight to twelve canoes (with two people in each canoe). Three or four leaders or guides should be assigned to specific positions within the group of canoes. One leader should be at the front. No other canoe should be allowed to pass that leader's canoe. Position two other experienced leaders in canoes at the middle of the group where they can supervise and monitor the students in the canoes. The fourth leader should stay in the rear of the group to act as a sweeper and to ensure everyone's safe passage.

Leaders should be selected on the basis of their canoeing experience, their knowledge of the river, and their demonstrated ability to control a group of four canoes (eight young people). Each leader's canoe should be equipped with a first aid kit and a set of ropes with ring buoys that can be thrown to people as lifelines. Before your trip it's best to take the leaders on a trial run down the river to build their knowledge of the river and give them experience communicating with one another while canoeing.

PRE-TRIP TRAINING

Pre-trip training in an indoor facility is highly recommended for both students and staff. Make the pool training part of the whole trip package. Lay out the rules of the trip. Go over the use of life jackets. Give basic instruction in all aspects of canoeing, including paddling and righting a capsized canoe. The pool setting provides opportunity to test swimming skills and teach safety techniques in a controlled setting.

The training process gives insight into the teachable attitude of each student. The pool training may eliminate some students from the trip. If they won't take instruction in the pool, don't expect them to cooperate when everyone is moving down a river.

WATER SPORTS WARNING

Youth leaders should not sign a group waiver form that takes responsibility for all the students. When the river company or outfitter requires a waiver releasing it from responsibility, get copies of the waiver form prior to the trip. Give the forms to the students to be signed by the parents.

Recently a youth leader and the ministry employing him were sued by the family of a young person killed during a rafting trip. The leader had signed the river company's waiver form at the site just before the group left on the trip. His signature indicated that he and his ministry organization would take responsibility for the students. Lack of planning and a spur-of-the-moment decision caused the youth leader to take on a responsibility that belonged only to the parents.

RAFTING AND TUBING

Whitewater rafting has gotten a great deal of scrutiny from the insurance industry because of several fatal tragedies. Although these accidents were on dangerous class 5 rivers, every rafting outfitter has been placed under the same scrutiny. The job of the youth leader is to find a top-notch outfitter with good equipment to guide the youth group.

Many of the safety guidelines listed for canoeing also apply to rafting. Listen to the instructions of your outfitter. Let the company do the work and provide the safety precautions for which you are paying.

Be sure to check the liability insurance policy of your church or youth ministry to see if it excludes whitewater rafting. Work with the outfitter to make sure each participant is adequately covered with insurance.

Tubing should be restricted to slow, lazy rivers on hot summer days. It is impossible to control a tube or protect one's arms and legs (and butt) in a fast river with rocks. Even with a helmet, the risk of injury in attempting to tube a fast river is beyond what's acceptable for a youth ministry. Even on a slow river everyone must be a strong swimmer. The staff must know the river (Is a waterfall ahead?) and be strategically placed throughout the group as specified in the canoeing instructions.

BOATING AND WATERSKIING

Late one afternoon at a Christian camp, a full-time, experienced staff person at a water recreation area broke his own safety rules. He'd been driving a water-ski boat for over four hours (violating rule #1) and was feeling the fatigue. This last ride was a good friend who was asking for more and more challenges. He accommodated the requests of his friend and took him off the normal ski course (rule #2). He drove the boat into an area of the lake restricted for use only by sail boats (rule #3) and crashed his motorboat directly into a sailboat.

The occupants of the sailboat had seen him coming and dove off the boat into the water. One young woman from the sailboat was surfacing as the motorboat passed through the area. The propeller caused deep lacerations on her back. The driver of the motorboat immediately switched into the emergency-response mode in which he'd been so thoroughly trained. Miraculously the young woman recovered fully from her serious injuries.

The camp staff's review of the accident determined the highly trained, mature leader who'd been driving the boat had been the victim of fatigue. He was so familiar with the waterfront that he'd overlooked the risks of skiing outside the designated areas. He got caught up in his desire to please a friend who wanted to push the limits of his skiing ability.

That staff leader is like a lot of youth ministers I know. He was diligent and hard working, putting in long hours without relief. He was highly motivated and didn't seem to know when to quit. He was also highly relational, eager to meet his friend's request. In this situation those strengths became his weaknesses. Fortunately the young woman's remarkable recovery freed him from carrying an enormous weight of guilt the rest of his life.

BOATING SAFETY

If a mature professional can experience a safety lapse, it serves as a warning to the rest of us who engage in boating activities only occasionally. If your youth ministry is going to use a boat for some activities, you're responsible to make sure it meets basic safety requirements. Whether you're using a boat borrowed from a friend or one owned by a camp you're using, be sure you've checked out the boat and its driver before you trust your students to step on board.

- Know the capabilities of your boat and motor.

- Know your fuel tank capacity. Monitor the gas level frequently so you are not stranded.

- Don't overload your boat. Balance your load.

- Have firefighting and lifesaving equipment always ready for use.

- Obey all boating laws and regulations.

- Have personal flotation devices for every person in the boat. This is the law.

- All children must wear life preservers. Everyone must wear them in rough weather.

- Prepare for emergency routines—fire, man overboard, bad leaks, motor breakdown, storm, etc.

- Learn distress and other marine signals.

- Carry proper charts and a magnetic compass.

- Have at least one person on board prepared to serve as emergency copilot.

- Follow manufacturer's specifications for the number of passengers to carry safely.

- Make sure everyone in the boat is seated before the motor is started.

- Drive at slower speeds in unfamiliar waters to reduce the possibility of striking an unexpected obstacle.

- Watch for swimmers.

- Know the official storm signals and boat accordingly.

- When a storm seems likely, head for home without delay.

- Angle your boat toward high waves and reduce speed.

- Avoid unnecessarily fast, sharp turns.

- Don't take the risk of being swamped or capsized by high waves.

- If the boat capsizes, passengers should try to stay with it. The overturned boat can support quite a few people even if it is nearly underwater.

- In an emergency situation guard against panic. Calm cooperation and resourcefulness are required for survival.

WATERSKIING SAFETY CONSIDERATIONS

Waterskiing is an especially popular activity in many youth ministries. It gives opportunity to build relationships while sharing an exhilarating sports experience. It is most safely done in the context of an accredited camp, but other youth ministries use boats periodically in local settings. The boats may also pull young people on kneeboards and inflated inner tubes—variations that can involve more kids. The following safety considerations apply to all these.

- Know and follow the state laws governing boating and skiing.

- Ski in safe areas, free from shallow rocks and undesirable obstructions.

- Load the ski boat with enough forward ballast to hold down the bow and guarantee forward vision. The safety of the skier depends entirely upon where the boat takes him or her.

- Always have a trained adult spotter in the boat to watch the skier and communicate with the driver. Many states require the boat to have a rearview mirror in addition to a spotter. Check your state's requirements.

- Insist that all skiers wear legal life jackets. Know what the law requires.

EMERGENCY RESPONSE

There are three safe and effective ways to assist a drowning person:

1. Reaching—use a pole, a paddle, a towel, a tree branch.
2. Throwing—use a heaving line, a ring buoy, a rescue tube.
3. Wading—use a buoyant object and extend it to the victim. Keep the safety device between you and the victim.

When assisting a drowning person, never overestimate your own ability. Don't endanger yourself. Swimming out to a victim requires special training.

(American Red Cross, Basic Water Safety Manual)

- Review and use a standard set of signals for communications between boat and skier.

- Remember that the boat can slow down sooner than the skier can.

- When terminating a run, slow down gradually before cutting the engine, to protect the skier from being driven into the boat by his or her momentum.

- Watch for swimmers and other hazards when skiing near a beach. Stay away from congested or heavily traveled areas.

- Teach the skier to grab one ski and hold it vertically out of the water after a fall so other boats can more easily see him or her in the water. Do the same with a kneeboard.

- When the skier falls take him or her aboard from the lee side.

- Stop the boat motor (don't just switch to neutral) when taking a skier aboard.

- Never tow your skier through shallow waters at high speeds. A tumble could be hazardous.

- Never tow two or more tubes or kneeboards with students of significantly different weights or with different lengths of rope. The longer rope can decapitate the person holding onto the shorter rope.

- Terminate waterskiing well before twilight when visibility decreases.

- Inspect towlines and fastenings regularly for worn or damaged equipment.

REFLECT AND INTERACT

Stop and reflect on your experiences and decisions related to the safety of young people. Better yet, discuss these questions with your youth ministry team:

- Which of your regular summer activities needs more supervision and safety checks?

- Do you and your staff have the training necessary to engage in water activities safely? If not, how can you get such training?

- In what situations have you been too casual supervising water sports and activities?

WINTER SPORTS

CHAPTER 12

"Wake up, Jack! Steven is hurt. He ran into a tree, and he can't move."
I couldn't decide if the voice was coming from my dreams or from
reality. I opened my eyes to see a couple of guys in ski jackets and mit-
tens hovering over me, begging me to get up and come with them. I
asked Steven's location. I sent one of the young men to wake another
counselor from the group (I was just a weekend visitor). I gave the
students a blanket to wrap around Steven. I cautioned them not to
move him but to tell him I would be there as soon as I got dressed.

What time was it? I squinted through my sleepy eyes to see
3:00 a.m. flashing back at me. I knew I had to dress for cold weather.
The temperature had rarely exceeded zero degrees Fahrenheit all
weekend. It had to be at least 15 degrees below zero now. I prayed
for Steven as I dressed and asked God to show me what I needed to
do when I arrived at the accident scene.

When I walked out of the camp dormitory to the sledding
hill, I was surprised to find no one at the hill or near the tree where
they'd told me Steven was lying. After searching the area I returned
to the building to find Steven in his bed, surrounded by a roomful of
kids. They'd all been sledding in the middle of the night while the
counselors were sound asleep. He'd hit the tree headfirst, and the
impact had caused a temporary paralysis, making it impossible for
him to move for a few minutes. When the feeling returned he'd gotten up off the ground and walked to his room.

Steven lay in his bunk—sore, scared, and thankful the paralysis wasn't permanent. I was quite aggravated about the 3 a.m. sledding, but I was glad he wasn't still lying on the ground next to that
tree. I told Steven he needed to visit the hospital emergency room for
a check up. He said he was fine. That was teen-speak for *I don't want*

to explain to my parents why I was sledding at 3 a.m. when they get the hospital bill. He almost had a couple counselors convinced until I demanded he be taken to the hospital. To my amazement Steven suffered no serious damage or lingering side effects.

When the temperature drops and the water turns to snow and ice, youth ministry activities become even more exciting. Snow camps, winter retreats, ski trips, and ice-skating parties help youth groups enjoy the cold weather. But a winter environment filled with fast and slippery hard surfaces and freezing temperatures creates a unique set of safety concerns.

ICE SPORTS

For groups with access to indoor arenas, ice-skating is popular year round. In most of these situations, the regulations and supervision provided by the rink operators ensure an acceptable level of safety. But when the skating moves away from the rink and onto a pond or lake, keeping kids safe becomes more challenging. Here are some guidelines for safe skating:

- Check the thickness of the ice. The Red Cross suggests that ice should be at least four inches thick for maximum safety. Check the entire area you intend to use for sufficient thickness. The more people on the ice, the thicker it needs to be. Mark off as restricted any areas where the ice is not sufficiently thick.

- Look for hazards that stick out above the ice. Mark them so they can be avoided.

- Always have a safety device available that you can throw or extend to any person who falls though the ice. It could be a long pole or a lifeline with a buoy. Prepare for the worst and hope you never have to use such devices.

- If the ice starts to crack under you, lie down flat and spread your arms and legs far apart to distribute your weight across a wide area. Crawl toward the safer, thicker ice maintaining your prone, spread position. Do not stand until you are on solid ground.

HOW TO HELP SOMEONE WHO HAS FALLEN THROUGH THE ICE

- Don't go out onto the cracking ice to help. You may join the person in the cold water if you do. Extend an emergency device that the victim can grasp and hold onto. Use a long pole, a tree branch, a buoy on a lifeline, or an inner tube attached to a rope.

- Get something to the person to grasp quickly. The longer the victim is in the cold water, the less he or she will be able to function. Pull the victim to shore or get the victim attached to the rescue device and go for help.

- Coach the victim to remain calm and to reach forward onto the ice, using a swimming-type kick to push himself or herself up on the ice. The victim should stay prone onto the ice, distributing his or her weight, and then crawl or roll away from the hole in the ice.

- Get the victim into warm shelter and dry clothes as quickly as possible. Warm the person with a warm (not hot) shower, bath, or fire. Give him or her warm liquids, but avoid alcohol or caffeine. Wrap the victim in dry clothes, a blanket, or sleeping bag. Get medical assistance if possible.

MORE ICE PROBLEMS

Many youth ministers believe games on ice are even more fun than on solid ground. In addition to ice hockey, it's not unusual to see broom hockey, football, soccer, and all types of relay races on ice. The slipping and sliding make for great fun. The problem is the surface of ice—it's just like concrete. Falls can cause serious injury. If professional hockey players require helmets for safety, should kids participate in contact sports on ice without head protection? Even with helmets, the students face a greater risk of broken bones while playing on ice.

FUN IN THE SNOW

We were promoting our winter snow camp with a film clip that showed more than 20 people sliding down a tree-lined, snow-covered trail on 10 to 12 inner tubes that had been lashed together. It was like a raft trip through the woods over the snow. It looked like so much fun.

When we arrived at our camp, we were excited to duplicate what we'd seen on the film. The camp had the snow, the inner tubes, and the long, downhill runs. The camp director assigned one of his professional staff members to supervise our tube run. His rules were much different than what we had expected or wanted. He allowed only one person on each tube and only one tube on the course at a time. He placed spotters on the course and at the bottom to help riders exit the course and return up the hill. It seemed as if he was spoiling all the fun. In fact, when he was called away for some other task, we hooked three or four tubes together, piled as many people on them as possible, and took a merry ride down the hill. It seemed like a lot more fun.

Since that weekend we have used many camps that didn't have this professional supervision. We've had total freedom to do whatever we wanted with tubes, sleds, and toboggans. Left to our own rules, we discovered our camp director friend was pretty smart.

Most accidents on tubes, sleds, and toboggans happen when people hit other people—one body crashing into other bodies. Piling two people atop a tube for a run down the hill is great fun until a bump sends one person's head into the teeth of his fellow passenger or the weight of one rider lands full force on the skinny arm or leg of another. We liked to play chicken with the people who were standing on the track or crossing it. And we loved to spin people on the tubes and send them down backward—but we've seen people hit trees and other people because they had no idea of where they were headed and had no ability to change direction.

You have to ask yourself if it is worth the risk of injury to continue a no-restraints approach to tubes, toboggans, and sleds. Completely safe tobogganing, sledding, and snow tubing is impossible. But it's clear that most accidents happen because of the speed, the lack of control, and the exposure of arms, legs, and heads to collisions. To be safest, follow these guidelines:

- Have a straight, wide course free of hazards and obstructions (including people).

- Avoid using sleds and toboggans with metal runners or metal facing that could cut someone's skin.

- Allow just one rider on each tube and sled. Don't overload large toboggans. Have all riders go down the hill feet-first.

- Place staff leaders at the top and bottom of the hill to spot for students and to enforce the rules.

- Discourage the building of jumps on the run. Lifting into the air is the fun part; landing on the ground is the dangerous part.

SNOWMOBILES

Snowmobiles are excluded from many insurance policies because of the loose restrictions concerning their operation and the numerous accidents involving them. Many camps still run snowmobiles under their own insurance policies, allowing only qualified camp staff to operate the powerful vehicles. Helmets should always be worn. Both the driver and the rider should take safety precautions.

In an attempt to be creative, some camps use snowmobiles and tow ropes to pull campers across the snow on inner tubes, water-ski style. The snowy terrain, though, is less predictable than a water surface. As I researched this book, several youth leaders reported that young people from their groups had hit trees while on tubes pulled by snowmobiles. One student suffered brain damage. Check your insurance policy before using snowmobiles. If you have coverage, use only qualified drivers, wear helmets, and obey safety regulations.

DOWNHILL SKIING AND SNOWBOARDING

A youth organization recently had an embarrassing day in the legal system. They were being sued by the family of a young man who had sustained a serious back injury while downhill skiing with their group. What was unique about this legal proceeding was that the episode in question had been recorded on videotape by one of the youth group leaders.

The video clearly showed the young man was a novice trying to ski down a slope that was beyond his capabilities. He was skiing out of control and fell, injuring his back. The students and staff with him could be heard encouraging him to ski down this slope and laughing when he fell. As he lay on the snow, they quipped and joked with him about getting up to continue skiing. In the context of the accident, the comments took a different tone than was intended. The leaders sounded insensitive and unconcerned for his safety. The judgment went against the youth organization.

Here are some rules for safer skiing and snowboarding trips.

- A responsible skiing/snowboarding trip starts with staff preparations. The leader needs release forms and medical information for all participants. It is smart to have at least one alternate driver with the group in case a driver is injured during the day. If you are skiing several hours from home, finding another capable driver could be costly in dollars and time.

- Each person should be given a slip of paper with your name, the name of your group, and your cell phone number, which can be used by emergency personnel if the person is injured. Since ski trips often attract students who don't know the group or its leaders very well, they may not be able to identify the adults responsible for them when asked by medical personnel.

- Set a meeting time during the day (a 60-minute period) when everyone should check in with a staff person at a designated location. Set a quitting time and a meeting spot for departure. If possible have an adult at a designated location throughout the day. Show students the location, and tell them to come to this person if they need help during the day. This adult should know how to contact the leader if necessary.

- If you travel by bus, have alternate transportation available if it's necessary to take a student to a hospital emergency room.

- Instruct your students not to ski alone. Encourage skiers to stay together in small groups and look out for one another. Spread out your adult leaders among the various groups of skiers. Be sure that capable adult leaders are supervising the beginning skiers.

- In extremely cold weather, instruct your students to return to the lodge to warm up after a certain period of time or number of runs. Alert students to the signs of frostbite and warn them to get help from you or the infirmary before they develop a severe condition.

- Snowboarders need to wear helmets and wrist guards. Eighty percent of snowboarding injuries involve wrists. Make sure boots fit tightly and comfortably. Proper clothing is needed for warmth and protection from wetness. Make sure all skiers wear goggles to protect their eyes from snow and ice and from damage caused by the sun.

- Don't let any of your more skilled skiers/snowboarders take other students to trails that are beyond their skills. Ski and board with the students who are learning until they can improve. Remember that the injury rate rises rapidly near the end of the day when people are tired.

• The Snow Parks at the mountains are very popular (thanks to the X-Games). No student should be allowed to board there without the leader's permission—based on the student's skill and experience. Review the safety code. Let your experienced skiers present the safety code to the group.

SKIER/SNOWBOARDER RESPONSIBILITY CODE

1. Ski under control and in a manner that allows you to stop or avoid other skiers or objects.

2. When skiing downhill or overtaking another skier, you must avoid the skier below you.

3. You must not stop where you obstruct a trail or are not visible from above.

4. When entering a trail or starting downhill, yield to other skiers.

5. All skiers shall wear retention straps or other devices to help prevent runaway skis.

6. You shall keep off closed trails and posted areas and observe all posted signs.

FOUR MAJOR CAUSES OF SKIING INJURIES

You can help your group have a much safer skiing experience if you are aware of what causes most ski injuries. Most skiing accidents can be attributed to one of four primary causes:

1. INADEQUATE INSTRUCTION

The goal of basic ski instruction is to teach skiers how to control where and how fast they're going and to learn how to stop. Every beginning skier needs instruction. The responsible leader must provide that instruction either through professional lessons at the lodge's ski school or from capable volunteers in the youth group.

Most injuries at a ski mountain involve beginning skiers, and many of them occur on slopes that are much too difficult for a beginner to handle. First-time skiers cannot be taken to the top of the mountain and turned loose to learn on their own. The throw-'em-in-the-deep-end method of teaching people to swim or ski is much too risky for a youth ministry leader.

Once I took a young man skiing who had never skied before. I was impatient and didn't want to spend all morning on the bunny slope. He was young and athletic, and I was confident I could teach him on the way down the hill. Looking at the trail map, I found some green trails (easiest) on one side of the mountain. When we left the chair lift at the top of the mountain, I discovered all the green trails were closed. I'd not taken time to check the condition of the trails before I took this novice skier up on the chair lift. Only blue (difficult) and black (expert) trails were open.

The trip down was a real disaster for him. Falling constantly drained all his energy and confidence. Within 15 minutes he hated skiing. After he took a nasty fall, I realized the danger I'd put him in and flagged down a ski patrol. They called a sled to take him to the base of the mountain and gave me a well-deserved reprimand. I spent the rest of the day on the bunny slope with him, rebuilding his confidence and teaching him the basics.

The same pressure is applied to many young people by friends who have more skiing experience. They take their friends into danger, accidents happen, and someone gets hurt. Then the leader gets to spend the rest of the day at the first aid station or the hospital emergency room. Prevent these accidents by demanding that new skiers stay on the bunny slope until they demonstrate the ability to ski under control. Some leaders require new skiers and snowboarders to buy a restricted ticket that limits them to the beginner slopes. Only when they demonstrate their improved ability are they allowed to upgrade the ticket.

2. POOR PHYSICAL CONDITIONING

Learning to ski can be very hard on young people who are not physically fit. Not everyone is ready for the rigors of skiing. Strong leg muscles and ligaments are needed to withstand the forces of a fall.

Stamina is needed to keep you from tiring quickly. Weaker people sustain more injuries. Either prepare your non-athletes prior to the trip, or keep a staff leader nearby to monitor them while they ski. Fatigue plays a big part in skiing and snowboarding injuries. Know when to encourage students to stop and rest.

3. EQUIPMENT ISSUES

Good equipment, properly fitted and adjusted, reduces the possibilities of injury. Resist the temptation to save money by borrowing equipment for new skiers or snowboarders rather than renting it. The fit of the boots, the length of the skis and poles, and the release setting on the bindings are crucial to safety and comfort. When young people rent equipment, remind them to be honest about two questions they'll be asked—their weight and their skiing ability. Their answers will determine how much the bindings holding the boots to the skis will be tightened. They shouldn't be embarrassed or pressured into giving information that isn't true. A dishonest answer can result in a broken leg when the ski doesn't release properly from the boot after a fall.

4. POOR JUDGMENT

Beginner skiers have little conception of how great a hazard speed can be. The key to safety is skiing under control. Most accident victims tell the same basic story. "I just started going faster and faster. I didn't know how to stop." Or "My skis got crossed and I couldn't control where they were going."

Poor judgment also causes people to keep skiing when they are exhausted. The last run of the day is notorious for accidents. Fatigued skiers grow careless or unable to control their speed. Be careful not to criticize youth who say they are tired or want to quit for the day. Your comments may push them to ski beyond their physical limits. The leader bears some responsibility for any accidents to students not given an opportunity to rest or call it quits.

After a full day of skiing with a group of young people, the trip home offers some additional safety challenges. The parking lot of the ski area can be hazardous. Tired students with aching feet don't always pay close attention to traffic. Vehicles with snow or winter dirt on the windshield don't always have clear visibility, especially in the fading light of late afternoon. People are standing by their vehicles changing clothes and loading equipment. Give special attention to your group and to others around you to avoid any parking lot mishaps. Be sure your driver for the trip home is alert and rested.

REFLECT AND INTERACT

Stop and reflect on your experiences and decisions related to the safety of young people. Better yet, discuss these questions with your youth ministry team:

- Which of your regular winter activities needs more supervision and safety checks?

- How often have you had kids hurt in winter activities? What could have been done to prevent the injuries?

- In what situations have you been too casual supervising winter sports and activities?

HIGH ADVENTURE

CHAPTER 13

Lenny slammed his bicycle down on the pavement of the roadside parking lot. Walking quickly past the picnic table covered with sandwiches and drinks, he cursed everyone and everything in his path. Just two-and-a-half days into an eight-day, 400-mile bicycle trip, Lenny was coming apart. Upon reaching the other end of the parking lot, he announced that he was going home... and started walking.

> **THE SAFETY FACTOR**
>
> While this chapter will help you consider some specific safety issues involved in various high adventure activities, it does not provide a comprehensive presentation of the training necessary to engage in these activities.

I laughed and calmly ate my lunch waiting for Lenny to turn around. When he was almost out of sight, I realized he was serious. My legs felt like Jell-o, but I ran down the road in pursuit. Lenny had no idea where he was or where he was going (a perfect illustration of his life). He was like a ticking time bomb rolling down the road. Nearly a mile later I finally cornered him against a barbed wire fence and attempted to defuse him.

The peace treaty we negotiated was only temporary. Every day something exploded in relation to Lenny. He collapsed from heat exhaustion because he insisted on wearing his jeans and jacket while riding. He sabotaged his own bike. He was in a fight almost every day. One incident came immediately after another student pulled Lenny out of a river when he appeared to be drowning. During a rainstorm he was riding so erratically that a staff leader separated him from the rest of the group. In anger Lenny pulled a knife and threatened him.

I'd thought a high-adventure trip would help Lenny turn his life around. Looking back, I wonder how we survived the week. I realize now that putting Lenny in a high adventure situation threatened not only his safety but also the well-being of the other students and staff.

WHAT IS HIGH ADVENTURE?

High adventure involves voluntarily putting ourselves into situations in the physical environment that challenge our physical and emotional toughness. Many high adventure activities are outside the boundaries of what most people would consider normal and safe.

High adventure includes mountaineering, ballooning, scuba diving, bicycling, motorcycling, spelunking, canoeing, kayaking, hang gliding, rafting, sailing, skiing, skydiving, rock climbing, trekking, and survival camping. You should check with your insurance carrier to determine which of these activities are covered by your liability insurance.

This chapter provides some general safety principles for including high adventure activities in a youth ministry. I've focused on bicycle touring and hiking/backpacking (plus a short note on rock climbing and rappelling) since these activities are often utilized in youth ministry. Check the chapters on winter sports and water safety for additional comments relevant to high adventure.

BEFORE CONSIDERING HIGH ADVENTURE

One word of advice fits all—high adventure activities should always be led by someone with appropriate training and experience. The smartest move every youth leader can make is to hire a certified trainer or guide to lead the youth group through one of these activities. If you are unwilling to spend the money to hire qualified guides, stay away from these activities. Don't rush ignorantly into any high-adventure trips without properly trained staff. It takes time to recognize the risks and develop competence and experience in your leaders.

By definition high adventure trips are risky and dangerous. That's part of what draws many youth leaders to use them. These trips are stressful on people—physically, emotionally, socially, and every other way. Even when following the strictest safety standards,

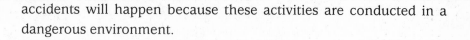

accidents will happen because these activities are conducted in a dangerous environment.

QUESTIONS WORTH ASKING

WHY DO I WANT TO INVOLVE YOUNG PEOPLE IN HIGH ADVENTURE?

It's important to consider whether high adventure is really the best way to accomplish your goals. The first step in planning any activity is writing a clear purpose statement for the activity. Why is this something you want your group to do? Perhaps you may think of a better way to accomplish your goal. Exposing your young people to the risks of high adventure may be unnecessary. Some youth leaders get involved in high adventure to enhance their own reputations. So ask, "Whose needs am I meeting here?"—and focus on the kids and your ministry with them.

WHO IS GOING TO LEAD THIS HIGH-ADVENTURE EXPERIENCE?

Do you have leaders that are experienced and qualified to safely lead this adventure, or will you hire professional guides? Quality leadership is the most important ingredient for both safety and success in high adventure.

WHAT TYPE OF YOUNG PEOPLE SHOULD PARTICIPATE?

Was it wise to bring Lenny on a weeklong bicycle trip? Definitely not. He was not ready—physically, emotionally, or socially—for the stress of a 400-mile bicycle trip with 30 of his peers. It's important to think carefully about the young people you intend to take on high adventure. So think it through:

- What is their physical health?

- What are their physical capabilities?

- Do they have drug or alcohol problems? High adventure is not the place to go cold turkey.

- Is their behavior at home irrational or unpredictable? High adventure will magnify it.

- Are they cocky, ego-driven, reckless, and afraid to fail? (If so, expect severe overreaction and poor response to leadership.)

- How do they act when under stress in their normal environment and routine? (The answer is a reliable guide for how they'll behave in high adventure situations.)

- How well do they take instruction?

- Are there scapegoat kids in the group—targets of peer abuse?

- Is there adequate time to screen students individually and determine how this trip might affect each person?

- What training and conditioning will you provide prior to the trip to prepare the students?

Lenny came on the trip at the last minute because I insisted on taking him. He wasn't screened using these type of questions. We didn't know until after the trip that he'd been kicked out of three schools for fighting. As much as we cared about Lenny, we were not prepared to help him, and we jeopardized the whole trip by bringing him along. The stressful situation only aggravated his problems. He was a major safety risk to himself and others.

WHAT IS OUR TRUE EXPOSURE TO DANGER THROUGH THIS EVENT?

Experience is vital for risk to be fairly and accurately assessed. Most dangerous situations are repetitive and can be predicted by experienced leaders. As a leader you must know what risks your students will face and decide if the event, activity, or trip is worth it. Those decisions are best made prior to departing, not in the heat of the moment.

WHAT IS THE QUALITY OF THE EQUIPMENT WE WILL USE?

It pays to go with a certified and trained outfitter who has quality equipment. It's seldom worth the investment for your group to buy specialty items for occasional use. High adventure requires top quality equipment. This is not the place for shortcuts or budget constraints.

HOW DO MY STAFF AND I REACT ON A TRIAL RUN?

Before taking any students, you and your adult leaders (with a qualified guide) should sample the high adventure experience you are considering. Seeing, feeling, and touching the activity for yourself will help you decide if it's best for the students you serve. Process the trial experience with your leaders, and use that time to teach needed skills. Debriefing is the primary teaching opportunity high adventure trips offer. With the help of your staff, students can learn valuable lessons about themselves regarding pressure, people, situations, fears, and faith.

WHAT IS OUR INSURANCE COVERAGE FOR THIS ACTIVITY?

Don't wait until you have an accident to ask this question. Your insurance agent doesn't want to be surprised with a claim for an event your policy excludes. If you're working with a reputable outfitter, you should be able to arrange special coverage to protect everyone involved. Be sure you have both medical and liability coverage for the trip. Seek the approval of your board or church leaders to confirm that you have sufficient coverage.

DO PARENTS KNOW WHAT'S GOING ON?

This is key. Parents need to be told specifics (both verbally and in writing) about what their young people will experience on this trip. Surprise is one of the major causes of lawsuits. Parents deserve prior knowledge. Put all the information on the permission form parents sign to give their consent for the activity.

BICYCLE TRIPS

The ending of our bicycle trip was always a four-star, goose-flesh experience for parents. The long double line of bicycles, each marked with a fluorescent orange flag, coasted down the paved road into the picnic area of the state park, marking the end of a 600-mile trip. Parents and relatives would rush from the picnic tables and line the road, looking for the special face of their child.

The bikers would roll through a gauntlet of video cameras and spirited applause before stopping to dismount and walk back into normal life. Mothers would cry. Fathers would beam with pride (especially for their daughters). We had arrived home safely. It was a memorable moment of relief and satisfaction. For me it was mostly relief.

Biking with young people has provided some of the great joys of my life and, sadly, the greatest sorrow I have ever known (see chapter 17). Genuine risk is always present. Despite the most thoughtful and strict safety standards, accidents can happen. Any leader considering biking with the youth group must count the potential cost.

I understand and respect parents who do not want their sons or daughters biking on public roadways. The setting is filled with many potentially uncontrollable elements. We cannot eliminate these dangers. Our goal as youth leaders is to provide a responsible atmosphere that ensures parents who do allow their children to ride on public roads that their kids are safer riding with our group than they would be riding on their own.

BICYCLING TRIP SAFETY ESSENTIALS

The essentials of safety remain the same in all bicycling situations when traveling on public roadways. There is no difference between a two-week tour and a one-day training ride near home; the following requirements still apply:

LEADERSHIP

As always, good leaders are the key component. One riding leader for every three to five student riders is the best ratio. A group of six students could be supervised adequately by one junior leader (experienced college-age or less experienced adult) and one senior leader (experienced adult).

A good leader is defined by riding experience, physical conditioning, basic leadership skills, and commitment to safety standards. The absence of any of these qualifications significantly raises the risk of accidents and injuries. Being responsible for the safety of biking students is not the place for on-the-job training.

RIDING GROUP SIZE

Ideal size for a biking group is six to eight people including leaders. Larger groups are more fun, but they create supervision difficulties, hinder communication, and are a hazard to other vehicles. Stay small...it's safer. The size of the entire group should be determined by the number of qualified leaders available and the capacity of your accommodations. Trips of 20 to 40 total people (divided into three to six riding groups) work best.

SAFETY EQUIPMENT AND PREPARATION

Before you hit the road with your students, make sure everyone is adequately equipped and prepared:

1. Helmets are an absolute must. Don't let anyone ride 100 feet without a quality biking helmet. Most fatal biking accidents are the result of head injuries. Accept no excuses: No helmet—no riding. Check the helmet of each rider to make sure it rests squarely on the head, protecting both the front and rear portions of the head. All chinstraps must be fastened and drawn tight when riding. The helmet should be comfortable but should not move up and down or side to side on the rider's head. You can always expect resistance from some who don't want to wear helmets properly or at all. Remind them they'll probably only need that helmet once during their life, but that one moment could be the difference between a long life and a short life.

2. Orange fluorescent flags on six-foot fiberglass poles provide added visibility. They can attach with a bracket to the rear axle of the bike or can be taped to a rear carrying rack. Flags, poles, and brackets can be obtained through bike dealers or many department stores for $2-5 each. Encourage each student to buy a flag for his or her bike, or provide the flags when kids show up. Quick-release axles make the flags easy to attach and detach.

Many students initially resist riding with these flags because they associate them with children's bikes. Admittedly, most serious adult bikers don't use flags. Still, the flag requirement is valid. The flag gives drivers earlier visibility of the bikers. Drivers moving at the speed limit will see your bikers three to five seconds earlier. That gives them additional time to adjust to your presence on the road by slowing down or giving you more space.

You can't make students ride with flags on their own personal time. You may not even want to use one during your personal riding. However, riding with a group sponsored by the church or youth organization and under your responsibility is a different matter. Provide the best possible safety. It may be the protection you need on the road or in a courtroom. When the leader is firm about requiring everyone in the group to use a flag, the resistance usually disappears.

3. Bicycle inspection should be required before any trip. Ask an experienced bike mechanic to help check the condition of each bike (especially tires and brakes) and make sure it's properly adjusted to run smoothly and easily. Students can also be counseled about the quality and condition of their bike (for example, weight, gearing, etc.) in light of the trip they are planning to make with the group.

4. Safety standards for your biking group should be printed and available for distribution to bikers and parents prior to the trip. Use the printed information as a basis for a verbal instruction about biking standards and practices for your group. Don't skip your safety standards orientation if a new student joins your group to ride. Don't assume the student knows how to ride safely. Someday you may be asked by a lawyer to describe what safety instructions you gave to a student who was injured while biking under your supervision. Fight the temptation to take shortcuts in safety training. Remember to get this safety information to the parents prior to the trip.

5. Selecting the route of the trip is best done by a scout team that tests several possible trips. The scouts should record road conditions, directions, and places of interest where bikers could stop during a riding day. Check specific state maps for recommendations about the best roads for biking. Often the state transportation department can supply that information and will warn you about narrow roads with high speed and truck traffic. Use the scout's notes to prepare a printed sheet of directions outlining each day's route. Written warnings can be given about dangerous sections of highway. The sheet can also list information about emergency phone numbers, medical facilities, and the day's destination (with phone number).

6. Training rides are essential to prepare students for the trip. Instructions on how to shift gears must be reviewed. If the planned route is through hilly or mountainous regions and the students live in a flat area, training needs to be strenuous and creative to prepare them for what they will face. Set a minimum number of miles students should ride prior to the trip. Be sure to enforce safety rules strictly on training rides.

BIKING SAFETY STANDARDS

Make safety your primary concern—for you and for the members of your group. Obey all traffic rules just as you would when driving a car. Ride single file just to the right of the solid white line.

THE WEAK LINK

High adventure tests the physical and emotional reserves of everyone participating. Sometimes the weakest participant is the adult leader of the youth group.

Physically Fit: The leader needs about twice the energy of the average youth participant. The leader gets the least sleep and expends the most physical and emotional energy dealing with problems. Taking a pre-trip with just staff will warn the leader of the physical preparation necessary to build sufficient stamina and will help remove uncertainty factors that can drain emotional energy.

Healthy and Rested: Leaders often get sick one or two days into a trip because they've kept an exhausting schedule prior to the trip. They are so busy taking care of last-minute details that they miss sleep and begin the trip vulnerable to the germs and viruses present among the students and in the trip environment. A sick leader can destroy the effectiveness of the trip. Plan ahead so you will get the details done two days prior to departure. Force yourself and your leaders to rest and sleep well in the days prior to the trip.

Communicate with the riders in your group. Group riding is different from riding alone. Riding behind another bike blocks your vision of road conditions. Use a "call system" to inform each other of any obstacles, safety hazards, turning, braking, or stopping. The lead rider calls out the message. Each rider should repeat the call until it is passed back to the last rider in the group. The last rider calls out any messages about approaching traffic so riders can maintain their safe, single-file formation as cars and trucks pass by. The call system is vital to avoid accidents, flat tires, and bent rims.

Be ready for dangerous road conditions.

- Avoid riding over potholes, large cracks, and grooves in the road. Any of these can cause a biker to lose his or her balance.

- In wet weather be aware of the additional time it takes for braking. Rain and water flying off the tires can impair vision. Slow down and put more space between the bikes.

- Constantly watch for changes in road conditions. Call out broken glass, sand, gravel, dead animals, and all debris on the road.

- Watch out for steel grated bridges (wet or dry). Bikes don't handle well on them. Slow down and ride cautiously.

- When in heavy traffic, anticipate hazards that could occur in a split second (such as a person in a parked car opening a door).

- Watch speed when going downhill. Spread out and put more space between bikes. Allow more time to stop. Watch for traffic lights and stop signs at the bottom of hills. Warn everyone riding behind you.

Never Overlap Wheels. Overlapping is the greatest cause of serious accidents in group biking. Leaders must be relentless enforcing this rule. Overlapping is when the front wheel of one bike is alongside any portion of the rear wheel of the bike in front of it. In this situation the wheels are so close together that any sideways movement by either bike can cause the wheels to touch. Even the slightest brush of wheels can cause a rider (usually the rider following) to lose balance. Always keep a distance of at least two feet between the back tire of one bike and the front tire of the following bike. This distance must be increased in hazardous conditions such as steep hills and wet roads. Riders must consistently and loudly call out braking and stopping to prevent bikers that follow from overlapping.

Ride as a Group. Stay together as a group in all circumstances. Find a pace everyone can keep. Don't let the group be separated by large gaps of space. Make all turns or lane changes as a group. Move like a caterpillar with the lead rider and rear rider checking the approaching traffic and calling out directions. Use hand signals to warn vehicles of your intentions. No one should be turning or changing lanes apart from the group. Move through traffic lights and intersections together as well. The senior leader is best positioned in the last spot of the line where he or she can see the entire biking group. An additional leader can take one of the first three positions in the line.

Allow No Stupid Moves. What may seem safe when biking alone is not safe for group riding. No riding without hands on the handlebars. No drafting other vehicles. No weaving. No squirting water bottles at others, especially toward groups who are passing. (The natural response of the biker is to swerve left—away from the water and into the traffic. Don't allow riders to wear headphones, listen to iPods, or use cell phones while riding. Hearing is key to bike safety.

Get Off the Road. When you stop for repairs, directions, food, or even in case of an accident, it is important to get off the road immediately. Every bike and rider should be as far onto the shoulder of the road as possible. If you stop where there is little or no shoulder, move to another spot where riders can safely wait off the road while the problem is addressed.

Severe weather is another reason to get the bike group off the road entirely. Fog, heavy rain, and lightning require a decision by the group leader. Think about how well drivers moving at highway speed will be able to see the group and avoid striking any of the bikers. Be cautious and get off the road immediately until the weather conditions improve.

Never ride in darkness. No group should be biking before sunrise or after sunset. Leaders should take note of sunset times and pull their groups off the road if they have not reached their destination. Take no chances in dusk light. Alternate transportation can be arranged. Be sure you have the phone number of your trip leader or the location where your group is staying (if you are outside cell phone coverage) so you can call for assistance.

Get off the road whenever the traffic conditions, the condition of the road, or a combination of the two factors gives you reason to believe a biker might fall into traffic or be hit by a vehicle. Cyclists never like to walk their bikes, but on a bad road, walking beats riding in an ambulance or a hearse. The leader must not be afraid to make this decision (no matter how unpopular) and stick with it.

SIGNS OF TROUBLE

When is it unsafe for a student to ride? A well-trained leader can recognize trouble by carefully observing student bikers. Here's a partial list of potentially dangerous situations:

1. **Fatigue.** Yes, everybody gets tired on a bicycle trip—but the leader needs to monitor bikers' fatigue and provide appropriate rest. When heads are consistently down and riders seem less alert, they are becoming tired. Fatigue makes bikers prime candidates for an accident. If students are not in good physical condition for the trip, arrange for them to ride only a portion of the day until they increase their strength. Fatigue is also the product of not getting enough sleep. Failure to enforce a curfew or allow enough sleep time can lead to accidents on the road during the day. The longer the trip (in miles or days), the greater the possibility that accumulated fatigue could affect the group.

2. **Faintness/Dizziness/Drowsiness.** This is a threat to a rider's balance and ability to react. Leaders need to remind riders to speak up when they are experiencing these symptoms. Hot days, bright sun, upset stomachs, dehydration, and medication can cause these

symptoms. Encourage students to speak openly about how they feel. Ask them directly if they feel any symptoms. Respond immediately by getting affected students off the road and into your support vehicle. Be especially careful of students using any medication that causes drowsiness.

3. **Dehydration and Heat Problems.** Riders should drink plenty of water while cycling to replace fluids. Every bike should carry one or two water bottles filled with water or a sports exercise beverage containing electrolyte supplements. Riders should take a drink every five or ten minutes and shouldn't wait to feel thirsty to begin drinking. The leader should remind students to drink as they ride. A reliable guide for detecting dehydration is the inability to urinate at least every two hours when actively exercising. When someone cannot urinate, his or her body is holding onto fluids. This condition is easier to prevent than to correct. Teach students this warning sign of dehydration and encourage them to speak up about how they feel.

Heat exhaustion is caused by the loss of important fluids and salt. The signs and symptoms are dizziness, pale skin, nausea, and rapid heartbeat. Treat victims by removing them from the heat source, sponging them down with water, and giving them sips of fluid fortified with an electrolyte supplement or salt. Be careful in the cooling process not to send them into hypothermia.

Heat stroke is far more dangerous and comes on much more suddenly. Common symptoms are confusion, irrational behavior, rapid pulse and breathing, hot and dry skin, and loss of consciousness. To treat this condition remove some clothing and moisten the body with cool water. Again, do not cool the body into a hypothermic state. Evacuation to a hospital is necessary.

4. **Hyperventilation.** When riders are climbing long hills, inhaling and exhaling heavily, they can develop a shallow breathing pattern that does not provide enough oxygen to their system. The faster they breathe, the less oxygen they get into their system. Hyperventilating persons may panic, feeling a form of suffocation as they gasp for air. The leader must get such persons off the bike and seated in a safe spot with their heads down between their knees. In ideal circumstances, the leader should put a paper bag over the victim's nose and mouth and instruct him or her to breathe deeply and

slowly. Lacking a paper bag, an inventive leader can use a bandana or a shirt tent-style or even cup his hands over the student's nose and mouth. The victim needs more carbon dioxide in his or her lungs to restore normal breathing. Have the victim rest until the breathing returns to normal and he or she feels confident enough to get back on the bicycle.

5. **Sunburn.** Moving through the wind, riders may not realize the sunburn they may experience. In addition to the normal spots you'd expect to be sunburned, special care should be given to protect the front of the upper legs, the back of the lower legs, and the ears, nose, and face. Long hours on the bicycle can numb a person to the power of the sun. Use generous amounts of sunscreen and sun block. Treat burns with aloe vera gel. Do not break blisters for fear of infection. Keep the affected area clean.

WHO CARRIES THE GEAR?

Bicycle-touring purists carry all their gear on their bikes in panniers, a set of luggage packs over the wheels. While transporting all our own gear may give us a feeling of self-sufficiency, the packs make a bike much heavier and harder to maneuver. If you have younger, inexperienced riders, it is wiser and safer to supply a support vehicle (van or small truck) to carry their duffel bags and sleeping bags.

The support vehicle also plays a crucial safety role. It monitors the riding groups by moving along the route in a leapfrog pattern—moving ahead and waiting on the side of the road for groups to pass by. If the vehicle is clearly marked with a sign or orange flag, it alerts motorists to the presence of bikes on the road and attracts anyone who has helpful information for the group leaders. The support vehicle is available to take aboard any biker who is injured or sick. It gives the group leaders better opportunity to respond immediately to anyone who needs medical attention for any reason.

MOUNTAIN BIKING

The popularity of mountain bikes opens additional cycling opportunities. The wider tires of mountain bikes give riders more stability and confidence. The rugged frame and tires enable bikers to ride through rougher road conditions without having to swerve into the road or risk falling. Mountain bikes are very appropriate for younger, less experienced riders.

Helmets should be required on all roads and trails. Scout trails in advance to ensure the level of challenge and danger (especially going downhill) matches the skills of the riders. The same training preparations and attention to danger signs for road biking apply to mountain biking.

Mountain bikes have also opened up new trip possibilities. In many areas old railroad beds are being renovated for bike paths. You can travel from Washington, D.C. to Ohio on an old railroad bed. The grade of the road is gradual and often runs adjacent to a river because it was built for freight train travel. Mountain bike trails offer trip opportunities off the paved road and away from the traffic. Many ski areas now open their trails for mountain biking in summer. The obvious advantage to such a trip is that it removes the traffic risk. The disadvantage is that bikers may be farther from medical help if it is needed. The safety concerns of a mountain biking trip should be treated like a backpacking trip on wheels.

BACKPACKING AND HIKING

The storm came over the campsite with incredible speed. The exhausted young people were just entering their tents and crawling into their sleeping bags after a long strenuous day. Several tents were pitched around the base of a tree.

Suddenly, before a drop of rain had fallen, lightning hit the tree. The crack of thunder shook the entire camp. The silence after the thunder was pierced by the hysterical crying of two girls from a tent near the tree.

Al, the youth group leader, had no idea what he'd see when he looked inside the tent. One girl lay in her sleeping bag, apparently paralyzed. The zipper of the sleeping bag had melted and been welded together permanently. Part of the metal zipper was attached to the skin of this girl's leg. The other girl lay beside her, stunned and unable to hear.

The tree the lightning struck was just five feet from where the tent had been pitched. The roots of the tree extended out from the base and ran directly under the tent. The electrical current had traveled through the roots and into the tent.

One of the volunteer leaders helping with the trip was a surgeon. He assessed their situation and sent a leader for medical help. Fortunately the campground was just off the hiking trail. Within an hour the young women were on their way to the hospital.

The girls suffered minor burns from the lightning. The paralysis only lasted for 30 minutes. Their hearing returned to normal. They

ON THE WITNESS STAND

I can still hear Chrissy screaming. She was 30 feet below me, hanging on a rope by her hair (literally). Chrissy was one of 15 students who'd accepted the challenge to rappel down a 70-foot cliff. I was leading the activity with Charlie—a ministry volunteer who climbs with ropes regularly in his work as a professional tree-trimmer. He had the equipment, the know-how, and the persuasiveness to talk me into offering this adventure to the kids at our camp.

Everything was going great until Chrissy's long hair came out of her bandana and became entwined in the rope. (She was not wearing a helmet—a major blunder on my part). She panicked and abandoned her rappelling hand position to grab the rope any way she could to keep her hair from being pulled out of her head.

Charlie heard the scream and jumped over the edge Indiana Jones-style, grabbing an adjacent rope on the way down. It was extremely reckless but effective. He reached Chrissy, stabilized her position, and cut her hair from the rope with his hunting knife. Chrissy clung to him with a death hold as Charlie lowered them both to safety.

We laughed and bragged about the incident that night at our camp. It gave me a great opportunity to talk to Chrissy (a noted agnostic) about whom she was praying to while hanging on the rope. But I was a stupid, foolish leader who just dodged a major bullet. Charlie's heroic reaction had saved Chrissy from a major injury or death.

In a court of law, I'd have been asked lots of questions: What were Charlie's credentials to lead such an activity? Why didn't we use protective headgear? Why didn't her parents know she'd be rappelling down a 70-foot cliff when she went to camp with us? The questions would be endless, but the conclusion would be clear. I foolishly miscalculated the risk and allowed Chrissy to be in a situation that threatened her life.

were released from the hospital that evening into the care of their parents. Al had called the parents from the hospital. He said it was the most frightening phone conversation he'd ever had with a parent.

The awesome power of natural forces is always on display when a youth group hikes into the wilderness. When the power show becomes too intense, youth workers are often isolated from necessary services and professional medical assistance. Al and his group were fortunate to be camped near civilization on that memorable evening. They were thankful to have a trained medical resource with them.

Hiking and backpacking can be very safe, but the smallest problem can become major when medical assistance is hours away. Natural forces and wilderness locations are not to be underestimated as safety risks for youth groups.

Hiking and backpacking are different from simple camping. If a youth group wants a natural setting with some modern conveniences, a campground is the best choice, for it provides access to transportation and phones. But overnight hiking and backpacking trips that take groups into the wilderness and away from civilization require properly trained leaders.

BEFORE YOU HIKE: LEADER PREPARATION

Before taking a group into the wilderness the leader has some important work to do:

- Plan the trip with a high quality map.

- Arrange enough leaders to provide a 1:3 adult-to-student ratio. (Ten students with three leaders is a maximum number for a wilderness experience.) Don't overlook parents as potential staff leaders. If all the students going are female, it's still best to have a male staff member as part of the leadership team for the trip to discourage aggressive and obnoxious male campers the group might encounter.

- Find a trained medical professional (such as a registered nurse or emergency medical technician) to travel with you. At the very least one of your leaders needs extensive first aid training and experience.

- Take the trip yourself with your team of leaders.

- Talk with your team of leaders about potential dangers and work through some worst-case scenarios with them.

- Obtain and distribute information about contacting park rangers and local hospitals.

- Study the route of the trip carefully so you know where and how to find emergency help.

- Check the cell phone coverage for the trip and set up a contacting schedule with your support team. Make several trial runs with the system to make sure it is satisfactory.

- Prepare a list with your hikers' names and medical/ insurance information, and carry it with you during the trip.

- Provide a map of your route to an outside contact person who can alert authorities if you experience difficulties.

- Pack a fully stocked first aid kit. (See chapter 15 for suggestions on contents.)

Ted and several students from his youth group woke up in the mountains of Pennsylvania to find their campsite covered with fresh snow—the product of a surprise spring storm. They weren't prepared for the knee-deep snow or the windy, cold weather. Six miles from yesterday's drop-off spot and a full two-day hike from the spot where their pre-arranged pick-up would be meeting them, how would they survive these days without suffering frostbite or exposure?

Fortunately Ted and his crew had hired a capable guide to lead this trip. After two hours of difficult hiking through the snow, the group arrived at a paved road where a van was waiting. The guide had used his portable radio to call his support team and arrange the rendezvous. He explained later that he always had alternative plans prepared in case an emergency evacuation was needed. Thorough and careful planning averted what could have been a tragic disaster for Ted and his students.

STUDENT PREPARATION

Establish some standards of readiness to determine if students are qualified to participate on a wilderness trip. Make sure students experience some shorter, single overnight trips before accepting them for a multiple-day trip that takes them far from civilization. The short trips will provide a clear measure of whether they have the physical fitness and emotional stability necessary for a longer, more challenging trip.

The most crucial piece of equipment on a hiking trip is a good pair of boots or shoes. They must be properly fitted and comfortable to avoid painful and crippling blisters. Students should be wearing them regularly prior to the trip.

Prior to the trip check the quality and reliability of any equipment students are required to furnish. Each student's backpack should be inspected and packed with a staff leader present to ensure proper items are included and unnecessary items are left at home.

If you have any reason to suspect students are attempting to smuggle alcohol or drugs on the trip, pack the bags two days prior to the trip. The leader can store the fully packed bags under his or her supervision and release them when they arrive at the drop-off spot.

ON THE TRAIL

As you enter the woods and begin to hike the trail, be sure to sign in at the box provided by the forest ranger. This is not the place for jokes or phony information. Respect and use this safety procedure. Obey the laws and regulations of the park. Take time to familiarize your group with the rules and demand their compliance. Other than pocketknives, small axes, and saws, no one should be carrying any type of weapon (firearm, machete, etc.)

Never camp . . .

- Under tall trees that could attract lightning or whose branches or limbs could fall during a windstorm. Woodsmen call such trees "widow-makers."

- In tall dry grass. A fire could ignite and spread rapidly to engulf the tents.

- In a gully or canyon. A flash flood could start miles away and rush down to wipe out everything in its path.

- Near or below the high-tide line on a beach or the shoreline.

- Under an overhanging cliff or bluff. A rockslide or avalanche could bury your campsite.

- Atop the roots of large tall trees (remember Al's lesson). Electricity from lightning that hits a tree can travel through the root system and burn anyone or anything it contacts.

WATER PURIFICATION

This is a necessary task, regardless of the water's source. Your first experience with vomiting and diarrhea caused by impure water will convince you. Purification can be accomplished by three methods—boiling, filtering, and chemical treatment. The chemical treatment is quicker than boiling and more reliable than filtering.

CLEANING DISHES AND UTENSILS

Campers can come down with diarrhea when dishes are not thoroughly cleaned or adequately rinsed to remove all soap. Diarrhea is not only inconvenient and uncomfortable; it can trigger severe dehydration.

FOOD IN THE CAMP

Never store food (even the smallest quantities) in tents where campers are sleeping. Animals of all sizes and types will find a way into that tent perhaps with tragic results. The most obvious and serious danger is bears. But even in bear-free areas, caution must be taken to discourage common visitors, such as, porcupines and raccoons—a nighttime encounter in close quarters with either of these animals could cause injuries. All food should be placed in a special food bag or backpack and hoisted up where it cannot be reached from the ground or by climbing the tree. Take extra care to ensure that students don't take snacks to bed with them. The scent of food, even just crumbs and opened wrappers, is enough to attract some unwanted visitors.

FIRE

Almost every young person loves to build a fire and play with it. A leader must supervise the fire at all times. Ignore the pleading of the students and keep the fire small. Build it in an open area (no overhanging trees), in a pit, or inside a ring of rocks to protect it from spreading. Never use rocks from a lake or stream. They may explode when heated. Make sure the fire is safely away from any tents or tarps. Before you leave the campsite, extinguish the fire completely. Water down any partially burned logs that might ignite after you leave.

HIKING IN DENSE UNDERBRUSH

Teach young people to watch for branches and brush that might swing into the face and eyes of someone walking behind them. Never stand or walk on loose rocks or logs if you can step over or around them. Falling can cause severe sprains or fractures.

GROUP-MINDEDNESS

Hiking and backpacking with a youth group is not an individual experience. Every decision is a group decision. Every student should be within the sight of some staff member when on the trail or in the camp. No one should venture out of the camp area without a partner.

LOST

The group members should all be taught the international distress signal. The distress signal is three repeated sounds (whistles, etc.) or flashes (flashlight or mirror). The rescue group is to respond with two repeated sounds or flashes. It is good preparation to carry a whistle in your pack at all times. Teach young people to use the signal only in the event of an actual need.

HYPOTHERMIA

When a person's body is unable to generate enough warmth, he or she becomes a victim of hypothermia. Differentiating between mild and severe hypothermia can be difficult. It is easier to prevent than to treat. Hypothermia can be prevented by dressing appropriately for the weather, keeping the body and clothing dry, covering the extremities (head, neck, and hands), and wearing clothes that maintain insulating properties even when wet. Wet clothing or a cold wind on a body wet with perspiration can lead to hypothermia.

Hypothermia has two stages. A mildly hypothermic person will complain of cold and have difficulty performing simple motor functions. The person may develop the shivers, become apathetic, and his or her body core temperature can be as low as 95 degrees Fahrenheit. Move the person from the cold into a warm environment, then remove damp clothing or add warm insulation. Offer warm liquids and food.

Victims of moderate or severe hypothermia will exhibit slurred speech, stumbling, unresponsiveness, and decreased pulse and breathing. Body temperature will be below 95 degrees Fahrenheit. Cover the victim immediately. Do not allow the person to walk or move. Handle him or her gently. Get medical help. In all situations of potential hypothermia, respond to the signs and symptoms, even if the victim doesn't.

FROSTBITE

Frostbite is caused by the restriction or stoppage of blood circulation to the extremities such as fingers and toes. The loss of circulation allows the fluid in the tissues to freeze when the surrounding temperature is below 32 degrees Fahrenheit. The main symptom is white skin that is waxy and hard to the touch. The area may feel intensely cold and numb. Primary treatment involves preventing further damage to the frozen tissue from thawing and refreezing. Give the victim plenty of fluids. Warm the body part only if it is not going to bear weight and will not refreeze. Do not rub or massage the area. Take the person to a hospital.

INSECT BITES AND STINGS

Unless the victim suffers an allergic reaction, bites and stings are usually more painful than serious. For bee stings use a knife edge to scrape out the stinger. Using tweezers or grabbing the stinger with fingernails may squeeze more venom into the sting area. Wash with soap, and apply an anti-sting lotion. If the victim suffers an allergic reaction, keep him or her calm, give an antihistamine, maintain an open airway, and transport the person to a hospital. People who know they are allergic should carry an Ana-Kit or an EpiPen that contains a pre-measured injection to fight the reaction.

POISON OAK, POISON IVY, AND POISON SUMAC

Learn to identify poisonous plants. Poison oak and poison ivy both go by the rule "leaves of three, let them be." The plants secrete a noxious oil that severely irritates the skin when transmitted by direct contact and contact with contaminated clothing. Within one or two days of contact, skin will burn, itch, and sometimes blister. If you suspect contact with such plants, remove the contaminated clothes and wash separately. Wash the skin with strong laundry soap and warm (not hot) water. Wipe down the affected area with rubbing alcohol. If a rash develops, avoid scratching, for open blisters could lead to a secondary infection. Apply cold compresses and a lotion containing hydrocortisone.

ROCK CLIMBING AND RAPPELLING

If you can't hire or recruit a certified and experienced instructor, you and your youth group shouldn't even attempt rock climbing or rappelling. Most insurance companies no longer cover these activities. Check your policy.

When looking for a guide, ask about your potential guide's training—National Outdoor Leadership School (NOLS) is probably the best—and his or her experience leading groups. Check the person's references; don't take any shortcuts. The lives of your students will be in the hands of this person. Be sure to take your staff on a pre-trip experience with the guide to get a clear understanding of what's involved.

Despite the best training and equipment, rock climbing and rappelling accidents *do* happen. Recently, a youth organization suffered a fatality when the professional guide did not tie the rope to the harness correctly. It was something he'd done successfully thousands of times. In this type of activity, a small mistake can mean severe injury or death.

REFLECT AND INTERACT

Stop and reflect on your experiences and decisions related to the safety of young people. Better yet, discuss these questions with your youth ministry team:

- What experiences or training have leaders on your youth ministry team had with high adventure events?

- In what ways would a high adventure event be a positive or negative experience for the kids in your group?

- How would you determine if a young person is ready for a high adventure experience?

MOST ACCIDENTS HAPPEN AT HOME

CHAPTER 14

It was Friday night and time for "Death Tag!" With all the lights off, the students hid throughout the church building. The youth director searched for them, armed with butterscotch candies he would throw at them to "kill" them. In past games one student hid in the rafters above a false ceiling. During the game he slipped off the rafters and crashed through the ceiling. This night a young man was fleeing through the basement and ran into a water pipe, bursting the pipe. Try explaining that to a church trustee.

Most youth ministers acknowledge the need for safety when our groups are climbing a mountain or canoeing a white water river. But when the setting is our church building and regular weekly meetings, we feel much more relaxed and complacent on safety issues. Like the experienced waterskiing instructor who broke his own safety rules (see chapter 11), the scenery is so familiar that we're blinded to the hazards and risks.

FACILITY HAZARDS

Safety agencies tell us most accidents happen at home. If that is true the regular meeting place of our youth group is the "home" that we should be making safe. Often, we don't see the hazards right in front of us each week. Here are a few questions to consider:

- Are there smoke detectors and fire extinguishers in the building? Without looking, do you know where they are? (Are the extinguishers hidden to keep our kids from fooling with them?) Is there fire emergency equipment in the kitchen?

- Is there a phone to use in an emergency? Are emergency phone numbers posted near it? Is your cell phone battery strong and ready for action?

- What access do students have to balconies and high places in the church building? Can they get onto the roof or fire escape? Falls are a common reason for serious accidents and injuries.

- Is the recreation room or gym outfitted with safety equipment, such as, protective mats at the end of the basketball court?

- Is there a well-stocked first aid kit available?

TEEN VEHICLES

The church parking lot can be a dangerous spot for your kids. As we recognized in our discussion of teen drivers in chapter 7, teenagers always seem to find something exciting (and dangerous) to do with motorized vehicles. Last summer one group had a lot of fun "surfing the hood" of the cars. Several students would stand "surfer style" on the front hood as the driver whipped around the parking lot. The driver would accelerate and brake, trying to make the surfers lose their balance. Our family was asked to pray for one young man who lay in a coma after he was thrown from the hood and hit his head on the pavement.

A youth leader can't wipe out the fascination teenagers have with motorized vehicles. These games will come and go. Students will be hurt. We can't control what students drive to our meetings, but we can monitor vehicle-related activity that goes on when they are under *our* supervision. For more on this subject, see chapter 7.

DANGEROUS GAMES
FOOD GAMES

Have you heard about Chubby Bunnies? You may know this game by a different name. Students compete to see who can fill their mouths with the most marshmallows and still say a phrase like "chubby

bunnies." Marshmallows are added until a competitor drops out—
and the last remaining competitor is declared the winner. Hearing
students slurring their responses as slobbery food drips from their
mouths can be very funny. But can you recognize the danger? Gasp-
ing for breath, a piece of food could be drawn into the windpipe,
causing the person to choke.

A 12-year-old girl died playing this game at her elementary
school in suburban Chicago in 1999. A 32-year-old woman died playing the game at a town fair in London, Ontario in 2006. Both victims
died from choking on a marshmallow particle.

We should give special scrutiny to any game that involves
forcing large amounts of food into a person's mouth. We used to hold
pizza-eating contests where guys would eat a triangular slice in less
than 10 seconds. It can't be healthy or safe for young people to ingest
large amounts of food without chewing it. Games in which food is
dropped or shot into someone's mouth are also dangerous because
of the risk of choking.

CHOKING GAMES

A terrible game sometimes called "Blackout" has received plenty of
publicity. In this activity students choke each other or themselves
to get a head rush when the flow of blood and oxygen are restored.
In some situations young people have killed themselves doing this.
There are reports of youth workers sponsoring this game at youth
meetings. It doesn't matter how popular such games are with teens.
Youth leaders must stop them.

THROWING GAMES

Throwing any objects in a youth group meeting needs to be carefully
monitored. Throwing activities need to be defined with a safe target,
specific objects to be thrown, and a clear starting and stopping point.
A "throwing" atmosphere can breed throwing just about anything
and everything—paper wads, pencils, wrapped candy, etc. Some of
the objects will be absolutely harmless. Others can be dangerous.
You can't expect young people to always know the difference and to
exercise good judgment.

HITTING GAMES

Be careful about any game that involves students tapping or hitting one another in any way. If a game involves hitting someone with a rolled up newspaper, who defines how hard students are to hit? Most students will hit gently and harmlessly. A student, frustrated or excited about the game, might blast a younger, smaller group member in the head or face. A particularly competitive student could easily lose control or get out of hand.

BEWARE THE EYES

Games that involve spraying anything in the eyes or face are strictly taboo—you might damage someone's eyes, glasses, or contact lenses. Sharp objects should not be used in games where a sudden, unexpected movement might cause them to strike a person's eye. Watch for blindfold games where someone might accidentally strike another person's eyes. I certainly felt different about my cops and robbers game (see chapter 9) when six hands started pawing my face and eyes, trying to pull a piece of tape off my forehead.

BEWARE THE TEETH

I've heard of students who required dental work after crashing to the floor face-first. They couldn't break their fall because they were wrapped in clear plastic wrap from feet to neck for the game Inchworm. If your game immobilizes a young person, you have to give them extra attention and protection.

WEAPONS BAN

We used to stage a fake assassination in our youth group meetings to set the stage for discussing violence. A stranger (arranged by our staff) would walk into the meeting and fire a starter pistol. A staff leader would be "struck" and would fall Hollywood-style as the stranger escaped. Although it was very dramatic and effective, it was not one of our better discussion starters. Today, I would never do any stunt involving a weapon at my meetings. Some young person at the meeting might pull out a real weapon to avenge what he'd just witnessed without knowing it was just an act. We live in that kind of world.

HIDE-AND-SEEK GAMES

The youth leaders I interviewed for this book told numerous stories about students (and leaders) hurt during hide-and-seek games in their church buildings. The game encourages students to find remote and unlikely places to hide. Teenagers are very creative (and competitive) and will find some interesting, and dangerous, hiding places. Some students have gotten stuck in crawl spaces; others have fallen through ceilings.

SCARING KIDS

Manny was new to the youth group. He liked coming with his friends, and everyone seemed to like him. One night the group set up a game where individuals would spend a few minutes in the dark, and then they'd be blasted with a bright strobe light so they'd see themselves in a mirror. The game really worked well on Manny. When the light flashed and he saw a face right in front of him, he reacted spontaneously and punched the mirror, cutting his hand. Manny's family sued the church and was awarded $25,000 in damages. If you decide to scare teens, be ready for a physical reaction or response. Don't have anything or anyone within reach that could cause injury.

ROUGH GAMES

Many youth groups love an occasional friendly game of tackle football (leader included). Neck, head, and dental injuries are the major risks. These injuries are much harder to repair than bruises or even broken bones. The most dangerous scenario is when young people

BEWARE OF GENERAL ADMISSION

Attending concerts and Christian music festivals is a favorite activity for many youth groups. But be careful about events with general admission seating. When waiting for the doors to open, the crowd can become aggressive about getting the best seats. Don't allow your students to run into the hall to get their seats. If they fall, they could be trampled and seriously hurt. It is illegal in many cities to have large events in concert hall/stadium settings with just general admission tickets. If you find yourself in a potentially dangerous situation at a concert or special event, don't be afraid to voice your concern to security guards or people in charge.

of varying physical sizes and abilities are in the same game. The weaker and less skilled are at high risk when they have no protection. Without proper protection such heavy contact games place an unnecessary risk on the young people involved.

DISCIPLINE PROBLEMS

In an ideal world youth group students listen to their leaders and carefully follow every instruction. You and I don't live in that world. But when young people challenge your authority, it threatens the safety and well-being of everyone involved. The youth leader needs to stop such behavior before the problem spreads.

Picture a table of students and leaders in a camp dining room. If two people at a single table start throwing food at each other, how long before other students and tables get involved and start throwing food? The responsible leader must never be afraid to take charge by stepping in and gently but firmly reminding young people of the safety standards.

Sometimes silliness just gets out of hand—and in those situations our own self-discipline is tremendously important. I remember a fall weekend retreat when play with squirt guns led to throwing cups of water, which eventually advanced to students being doused with bowls, pitchers, and buckets of water. I was in the kitchen working with students who were on dishwashing duty. I was angered when some of them left their posts to join the water mania. I was also angered by the mess they made spilling water all over the kitchen floor.

When I'd reached my boiling point, I grabbed one of the little guys who had hijacked the kitchen faucet and forcefully picked him up and threw him out the door onto the steps of the building. Everyone got the message and scattered for cover. But I physically hurt this young man. I'd lost my temper and had to apologize publicly to the whole group later that evening.

Youth leaders must not hit, punch, fight, or in any way physically abuse any student. Actions like that may prompt legal action against you. Verbal abuse may be just as bad. Calling names and using sarcasm may win the initial battle, but these actions undermine your long-term ministry with that group or individual.

When you face a young person who is physically acting out, you may need to restrain him or her to protect the safety of others in the group. The force of the youth leader, however, must always be defensive and restrained. Many health and human-service organizations offer special training in ways to safely calm and restrain a person who is out of control.

SAFETY ISSUES AND DISCIPLINE

Do students leave your meetings and activities early or disappear for periods of time during the meeting? You can't erect a wall around your youth room to keep kids in, but you do have an obligation to the parents. Your response to this behavior is somewhat related to the age of the students, but anyone in junior high or high school is still under the authority and supervision of his or her parent/guardian. If parents think their kids are attending the youth group, the youth leader must tell them if those kids are not.

When a young person exits early, the youth leader should confront that person directly and let him or her know the action is unacceptable. The leader should also outline the obligation to the parents. If the student continues to cut out, the youth leader must inform the parents and work together to change the behavior.

DRUG AND ALCOHOL PROBLEMS

What would you do if one of your volunteer leaders had a strong suspicion that one young person regularly attending your group was selling drugs to other youth in your group? What is your safety responsibility when you provide the social meeting place for these transactions? Experience has taught me you can't turn your head and think the problem will go away. But you shouldn't jump to conclusions and condemn the suspected person without a thorough investigation.

If kids want to buy or sell drugs (whether on or off your turf), it's almost impossible for you to stop them. But you can take action. Confront each person suspected of being involved as a seller or buyer. Kids may lie to your face, but you can send a strong message about how you are going to fight the sale and use of drugs in the youth program. You can let them know they will be under your watchful eye. Explain that you will personally confront them and bring other significant people (like their parents) into the matter if you have any evidence of their involvement. Then keep your promises. It's another way to show you care.

Have you decided how you'll respond if students show up to your meetings or activities showing signs of drinking or drug use? Will you let them stay and sit quietly in the meeting, or will you ask them to leave? The youth ministry team needs to make this decision before an incident occurs. If you decide to let these students stay, what special precautions will the staff take to keep them from disrupting the meeting or hurting others?

You should not be handling these matters alone. Even though you may feel like it reflects poorly on your leadership, you need to share these issues with your superior or board leaders. Don't let them be surprised about a drug problem within the ministry when some bad news becomes public. Ask for their help and guidance. They share the responsibility with you. When appropriate, talk to parents individually. They should be informed about major struggles in the life of their young people. Your pastor or director can be of great help to you as you relate to the parents.

REFLECT AND INTERACT

Stop and reflect on your experiences and decisions related to the safety of young people. Better yet, discuss these questions with your youth ministry team:

- What injuries have occurred during the regular operations of your youth ministry that required a trip to the hospital?

- What lessons about safety in youth ministry did you learn from experience before you read this book?

- What "dangerous" activities does your youth group do right now that you don't want to change or eliminate? What makes it hard to change?

DEALING WITH INJURIES AND PROBLEMS

CHAPTER 15

My stomach was growling as I stood near the camp swimming pool with 50 students and adults waiting for the dining hall to open for dinner. Suddenly, a high school boy with surfer shorts came running toward us shouting at maximum volume. He ran right past us at full speed, through the open gate, and did a headfirst leap into the pool. Some people know how to make an entrance. He was probably hoping to impress a girl in the group. It certainly got our attention.

Only one problem—he dove into the wrong end of the pool. I could see his body halt dramatically when he hit the bottom of the pool. He rose to the surface with a growing trail of deep red blood streaming from his head. As he stood up and cried for help, we stood frozen by what we saw. A six-inch flap of his scalp had been folded back over his head. The pool water was turning red.

Are you ready for a moment like that? When you decide to work with kids, you must realize events like this will happen. This chapter will start you on the path of being prepared to respond when a young person needs immediate medical attention.

My wife Becky broke the stunned silence that evening. She ordered two guys into the pool to steady him. She sent someone running to the camp office to call for help and another person to get an armful of towels. When we got him out of the pool, we inspected his wound for any foreign objects and carefully put the flap back over

AMERICAN RED CROSS FIRST AID MANUALS
Much of the information in this chapter is drawn from first aid and safety manuals published by the American Red Cross. Their manuals provide much more extensive and complete information on first aid responses mentioned in this chapter. Every youth worker should register with the American Red Cross or a similar organization and receive first aid training.

his scalp. We applied pressure with the towels to slow bleeding. A car soon arrived, and we drove him directly to the hospital.

Remarkably (Praise God), the student was back in camp by the end of the night, with his scalp stitched back in place and no complications. Ironically, the next morning I was scheduled to speak to the youth group leaders about safety. Nobody skipped that seminar.

It was a huge relief to see that young man walking around the camp the rest of the week with no serious complications from his stunt. But my feeling of inadequate preparation for a medical emergency stayed with me.

Every youth minister I know has a deep desire to help people who are in need. One way each of us can do that is by taking the time to be trained and prepared so we can respond to physical needs in a medical emergency.

FIRST AID

Before you read any further, here's an important disclaimer:

> **The following information is not a substitute for certified first aid training that should be required of all youth ministry staff. This chapter will help you respond to some common problems and alert you to first aid techniques that should be learned from a qualified trainer or organization. This section should not be regarded as a replacement for seeking immediate assistance from a trained medical professional or medical facility.**

It's also important to be sure you keep your first aid training up to date. The recommended training for cardiopulmonary resuscitation (CPR) and respiratory breathing was changed in 2007. Be sure to update your training and learn the new recommended actions.

I repeat—this information does not constitute training in first aid. Every youth ministry should train its staff in basic first aid and should have a professionally trained medical worker on site for trips and activities as often as possible.

WHERE DO YOU START?

With that warning in mind, administering basic first aid is often just a matter of common sense. The goal is to remain calm, assess the situation, call for help, provide comfort, and tend to the needs of the injured person as best as you can until help arrives. The basic principle of first aid is to do good if you can, while being careful not to do any harm.

BASIC STEPS OF FIRST AID

1. When an injury has occurred, assess the situation immediately for any additional possibility of injury to anyone else (including yourself). Make sure no one else will be hurt. Will you be in danger if you try to approach the victim to administer first aid? Don't put yourself in danger.

2. Do not move the injured person unless he or she is in an immediate life-threatening situation. Moving an injured person always risks additional injury that could cause permanent damage or death. If you have to move the victim, do it as quickly and carefully as possible. Avoid twisting or bending anyone who might have a neck or spine injury. (Note: In the opening story of this chapter, the young man who dove into the pool could easily have broken his neck. When he stood up on his own, we knew we could move him out of the pool. If he'd been motionless in the water, we would have had to make sure he could breathe while moving him as little as possible to avoid severing his spinal cord. That would have been an extremely serious and life-threatening situation.)

3. If the person has any of the following signs, call 911 or the local emergency number immediately. If possible one person should stay with the victim while another person makes the call. You should call 911 if the person...

- is unconscious.

- has trouble breathing.

- has chest pain or pressure.

- is bleeding severely.

- has pain or pressure in the abdomen that does not go away.

- is vomiting or passing blood.

- has seizures, severe headache, or slurred speech.

- appears to have been poisoned.

- has injuries to the head, neck, or back.

- has possible broken bones.

When calling 911, be sure to tell the dispatcher:

- the exact location or address of the emergency.

- your name.

- what happened to the victim(s).

- how many people are involved.

- the condition of the victim(s).

- what first aid is being administered.

The caller should not hang up until the dispatcher hangs up. He or she may need more information or may want to instruct you about how to care for the victim. After making the call, return to care for the victim until the ambulance arrives.

4. If the victim is unconscious, you should check three signs:

- Is the victim breathing? If not, you have a life-threatening situation. Check by putting your face close to the person's mouth and nose. Watch to see if his or her chest rises or falls. Check the airways for blockage. If the victim doesn't appear to be breathing, you must begin rescue breathing immediately.

- Does the victim have a pulse? Place your finger on the front of the person's neck in the groove next to the Adam's apple. If you feel a pulse but the person is not breathing, you will have to do rescue breathing. If you don't feel a pulse, you will have to do cardiopulmonary resuscitation (CPR). At that moment you'll be glad you sought training from the Red Cross or other organizations. Don't wait until you are in this situation to recognize your need for training.

COMMON CAUSES OF CHOKING

- Trying to swallow large pieces of poorly chewed food.
- Eating too fast, while laughing or while talking excitedly.
- Walking, playing, or running with food or objects in mouth.

- Is the victim bleeding severely? Check the victim's body from head to toe for signs of bleeding. Bleeding is severe when it spurts out of a wound. Control the bleeding by placing a clean dressing over the wound and applying pressure. A dressing can be any clean cloth or absorbent material (clothing, bandana, or sanitary napkin). Add additional dressings to the wound while maintaining constant pressure until the bleeding is controlled.

5. If the victim is conscious, ask him or her what happened. A verbal response confirms the victim's breathing and pulse. Look for any other life-threatening conditions. Talk to the victim or any witnesses to determine what care you need to give. Check the person for any problems. Don't move the victim or ask him or her to move. Watch for changes in breathing and consciousness. Look for a medical alert tag on the person's neck or wrist. If the injury or illness is related to the person's condition, call the number listed for help.

6. Stabilize any fractures or dislocations to prevent further discomfort or harm. If the fracture or dislocation needs to be set, this must be done by a trained medical professional.

7. Always treat for shock. Shock is a life-threatening condition even if the injury is not. Shock can be brought on by injury, poisoning, illness, allergic reaction, or even by seeing someone else injured. The signs and symptoms of shock are weakness, pale color, cool and clammy skin, irregular breathing, nausea, dizziness, and shivering.

If someone is in shock, the first task is to maintain the person's body temperature. If the outside temperature is cold, wrap him or her in an emergency blanket, sleeping bag, or extra clothing. If the temperature is hot, keep the person cool by creating shade. Always try to keep the victim insulated from the ground. The general rule is to keep the injured person lying down, comfortable, and resting with the feet raised (except in cases of head, neck, or back injury or possible broken bones). Control any external bleeding. Calm and reassure the victim. Although the person is likely to be thirsty, don't give him or her anything to eat or drink. If the injured person feels like moving or sitting up, don't restrain him or her.

8. If the person has a partially blocked airway and is coughing forcefully, let him or her try to cough up the object. A person who can cough is getting enough air to breath. Stay with the victim and encourage him or her to keep coughing. If the victim can't dislodge the object, call an ambulance.

A person whose airway is completely blocked will not be able to speak, cough forcefully, or breathe. The victim may cough weakly or make high-pitched noises. In that case have a bystander call an ambulance while you begin care. To open the airway quickly, stand behind the victim, wrap your arms around him or her, and squeeze tightly to give a series of quick hard thrusts to the victim's abdomen. Acquaint yourself thoroughly with the Heimlich maneuver.

DEALING WITH COMMON INJURIES

OPEN WOUNDS (CUTS AND LACERATIONS)

The best treatment for these wounds is cleansing with antibacterial soap and water. Then apply a clean, non-stick dressing, and secure it with adhesive tape. For serious bleeding, apply direct pressure immediately using a clean dressing. If you don't think the wound involves a broken bone, elevate the wound above the heart to slow the bleeding. When the bleeding stops, secure the wound with a compression bandage, and travel to the hospital for additional treatment. If the bleeding cannot be controlled, put pressure on the nearby artery (pressure point).

Treat for shock, which may be brought on by a loss of blood or a disruption in the circulation system. Infection is another major concern for all wounds. Always clean them with soap and water before applying an antibacterial ointment to prevent infection. After you have completed caring for the victim, be sure to wash your hands immediately.

SEVERE WOUNDS

If a part of the body has been severed or torn off, try to find the part and wrap it in sterile gauze or any clean material. Put the wrapped part in a plastic bag. Keep it cool with ice, but do not freeze it. Take it to the hospital with the victim. Doctors may be able to reattach it.

If an object is impaled in the wound of a victim, do not try to remove it. Place several dressings around it to keep it from moving. Bandage the dressings in place around the object.

Wounds that break through the abdomen may cause the organs to push out. Carefully remove clothing from around the wound. Cover the organs with a moist sterile dressing and cover the dressing with plastic wrap. Place a folded towel or other cloth over the dressing to keep the organs warm.

DENTAL

If the victim has had a tooth knocked out or damaged, place a sterile dressing directly in the space now vacant or damaged. Tell the victim to bite down carefully. If you can recover the tooth, it is important to get it replanted in the socket within an hour. Handle the knocked out tooth with care, picking it up by the chewing edge (crown), not the root. Do not touch the root part of the tooth. If possible place the tooth back into the socket. Have the person bite down gently and hold the tooth in place with a sterile dressing. If it can't be placed back in the socket, put it in a container of cool, fresh milk until you reach the dentist. If no milk is available, use water.

GENERAL CARE FOR HEAD AND SPINE INJURIES

- Minimize movement of the head and spine.
- Maintain an open airway.
- Check consciousness and breathing.
- Control any external bleeding.
- Keep the victim from getting chilled or overheated.

EYES

If a chemical or debris gets in a person's eye, flush the eye with large amounts of water. Be sure to flush from the inside corner of the eye (nearest the nose) outward, so the other eye is not also contaminated. Continue to flush the eye for 10-15 minutes, until you are sure the chemical or debris has been removed. Remove any thickened substance from the eye with a clean moist cloth. Flush the eye again. Do not put any medications in the eye. Cover the injured eye with a sterile gauze pad, and take the person to the hospital immediately.

BURNS

Minor burns usually don't require medical attention. Treatment, however, should be taken seriously. The affected part should be immersed in cool water to reduce pain and stop the burning sensation. Clean the area with soap and water, and apply a topical anesthetic. For more severe burns that blister or have deep tissue damage, the victim needs immediate medical attention. Don't apply ice directly to any burn unless it is very minor. Don't touch a burn with anything except a clean covering. Don't remove pieces of cloth that stick to the burned area. Don't try to clean a severe burn. Don't break blisters or use any kind of ointment on a severe burn.

SPRAINS

Falls or hits that suddenly twist a joint can cause sprains to wrists, knees, and ankles. Distinguishing between a break and a sprain is almost impossible without an X-ray. You should assume the limb is broken; then elevate it and immobilize it. Apply a cold pack to minimize swelling until the injured person can be examined at the hospital.

SPINAL INJURIES

Signs of spinal injury may include a change in consciousness, problems with breathing and vision, inability to move a body part, ongoing headache, nausea, vomiting, or loss of balance. When you recognize these signs, call an ambulance at once. While waiting for assistance, help the victim minimize any movement of his or her head or spine. Place your hands on both sides of the victim's head. Position the head gently in line with the body and support it in that position until medical personnel arrive. If you feel resistance or it hurts the victim as you try to do this, stop. Support the head as you found it.

SEIZURES

These may range from mild blackouts that could be mistaken for daydreaming to sudden uncontrolled muscular contractions lasting several minutes. Stay calm, knowing that most seizures last only a few minutes. Have someone call for an ambulance. Protect the person from injury, and keep his or her airway clear. If you see fluid—saliva, blood, or vomit—in the victim's mouth, roll him or her over on one side to drain the mouth and keep the airway open.

FAINTING

This is a temporary loss of consciousness often preceded by pale skin and perspiring. To care for fainting, place the victim on his or her back, elevate the feet, and loosen any restrictive clothing. Although fainting victims recover quickly with no lasting effects, fainting may be a symptom that signals a more serious condition.

ASTHMA ATTACKS

Asthma is a condition in which the air passages narrow, making breathing very difficult. The asthma victim makes wheezing noises when trying to breathe. Attacks can be triggered by an allergic reaction to food, medication, pollen, or insect stings. The attacks can also be brought on by physical activity or emotional distress. Most asthma victims carry medication to control an attack. Young people susceptible to asthma attacks should always carry that medication with them, especially on trips.

WHAT ABOUT HIV/AIDS?

The possibility of being infected with HIV/AIDS when offering first aid to a person who is HIV-positive is a concern to many people. But as long as appropriate precautions are taken, the actual risk of transmission in a first-aid situation is exceptionally slight.

AIDS is caused by the human immunodeficiency virus (HIV), which damages the body's immune system. The virus enters the body in three basic ways: 1) through direct contact with the bloodstream; 2) through the mucous membranes lining the eyes, mouth, throat, rectum, and vagina; 3) through the womb, birth canal, or breast milk.

The virus cannot enter through the skin unless the skin is cut or broken at the point of contact. Even then, the possibility of infection is very low unless there is direct contact for a lengthy period of time. Saliva is not known to transmit HIV.

The likelihood of HIV transmission during a first-aid situation is very low. Always give care in ways that protect you and the victim from disease transmission.

- If possible wash your hands before and after giving care, and wear gloves.

- Avoid touching or being splashed by another person's body fluids, especially blood.

- Avoid eating, drinking, and touching your mouth, eyes, or nose while providing care or before you wash your hands.

- Avoid touching objects that may have been contaminated with blood.

- Avoid handling any of your personal items such as combs or keys while providing care or before washing your hands.

- Be prepared with a first aid kit that includes waterless antiseptic hand cleaners and disposable gloves.

STOCKING YOUR FIRST AID KIT
BANDAGES, DRESSINGS, AND OTHER ITEMS

- sterile gauze pads in a variety of sizes, especially two-by-two and four-by-four inch pads

- roller gauze: Kling or Kerflex

- non-adhering dressing: Telfa pads (coat with antibacterial ointment or petroleum, and change frequently to prevent drying out and adhering to the skin)

- one-inch adhesive tape

- butterfly bandages or Steristrips assortment

- Ace Wrap: three-inch-wide bandage

- large compress: Use feminine hygiene pads

- assortment of cloth bandages

- moleskin (for the prevention and treatment of blisters)

- triangular bandage (for holding dressings in place, attaching splints, and creating slings)

- hand cleaner

EQUIPMENT AND ACCESSORIES

- tweezers

- needle

- single-sided razor blade

- bandage scissors

- irrigation syringe

- low-reading thermometer

- SAM Splint or wire mesh

- cold pack

- space blanket

- waterproof matches

- emergency phone numbers and money for a phone call

- bee-sting kit

- snakebite kit: compress, suction (use a Sawyer Kit)

- dental kit: oil of cloves, cotton pads, wax

- two pairs of latex gloves

- plastic bags

- small flashlight and extra batteries

MEDICINES AND DRUGS

Parental permission is needed for administering medication. Use the health form that parents submit to check with all students for any allergic history to any of these drugs.

PAIN RELIEF DRUGS AND TOPICAL APPLICATIONS

- Aspirin: mild analgesic; anti inflammatory, reduces fever; interferes with blood clotting; can cause nausea; don't give to children.

- Motrin: anti-inflammatory and moderate pain relief; may cause stomach irritation and nausea.

- Tylenol: for relief of minor to moderate pain such as muscle ache and inflammation; may cause liver damage in excessive doses; first choice for pain relief in many first aid kits.

ALLERGIC-REACTION DRUGS AND TOPICAL APPLICATIONS

- Benadryl: acts as an antihistamine, sedative, and anti-itch treatment. Use with caution; may cause drowsiness, constipation, weakness, headache, difficulty in urination, diarrhea.

- Ana-Kit: injection of epinephrine and Chlo-Amine tablets to relieve severe allergic reaction. May cause headache, anxiety, heart palpitations.

- Caladryl lotion: a calamine and Benadryl lotion to relieve minor skin irritations.

- Hydrocortisone ointment (2.5 percent): Steroid ointment for more severe skin reactions.

GASTROINTESTINAL MEDICATIONS

- Lomotil: controls diarrhea. Use only if the diarrhea compromises safety or ability to travel, since it is possible to introduce serious infection and start a fever because of bowel retention.

- Maalox: Neutralizes stomach acids and relieves indigestion. Can produce mild diarrhea.

ANTIBIOTIC AND ANTISEPTIC OINTMENTS AND SKIN PREPARATION

- Neosporin Ointment: Helps prevent infection in minor cuts and abrasions.

- Betadine: Use for topical cleaning of skin around the wound or before lancing a blister. If using to clean a wound, use a combination of 25 percent Betadine to 75 percent sterile water. Never use Betadine in a deep wound.

- Tincture of Benzoin: Prepares skin for application of adhesive.

OTHER DRUGS TO CONSIDER

- Cough suppressant: for example, Robitussin with codeine.

- Decongestant: for example, Afrin Nasal Spray (not recommended for use over prolonged periods or at high altitudes).

- Antibiotic Eye Drops: for example, Neosporin Ophthalmic Drops.

- Skin Care: for example, A & D Ointment, which soothes rashes and dry skin.

Be sure to check the first aid kit regularly to discard any out-of-date items. Design your first aid kid to fit your specific activities.

INFORMING PARENTS AND SUPERVISORS

Parents must be informed about any injury their child sustains while under the supervision of the youth ministry. Even a small injury should motivate the youth leader to meet the parents at the car when they come to pick up their son or daughter. A quick explanation of what happened and how the injury was treated keeps parents informed and builds confidence that their young people are being properly supervised.

If the accident is more serious and requires a trip to the emergency room, the parents must be called. It is better for the parents to hear from the youth worker directly before getting a call from a hospital worker calling to confirm insurance coverage or requesting permission to treat the injury.

There's no subtle or clever way to inform parents about an injury to their son or daughter. Direct and clear is the best style. Don't drag it out. They want to hear the bottom line—how their son or daughter is right now. Here is a sample conversation:

> *"Hello, Mrs. Jones, this is Jack Crabtree from the youth ministry at church. Please don't be alarmed. I'm just calling to tell you that Danny took a fall tonight in the church gym and hurt his arm. He is in good shape, but he's having a lot of pain in that arm. So we decided to bring him to the hospital emergency room for X-rays and treatment. We are here at the hospital right now getting him checked in. I just wanted to let you know what is happening."*

That's not too hard, since you know you're dealing with no more than a broken bone. You would stay on the phone to answer any questions the parents would have and give information about how they can find you and come to see their son. Let's try a more difficult one:

> *"Hello, Mrs. Collins, this is Jack Crabtree, from the youth ministry mission trip. I am calling to let you know Brian was injured about an hour ago. He took a pretty nasty fall here at the worksite. (220 miles from home) We're at the hospital right now. I don't know the full extent of his injuries, but the ambulance guys told me he is conscious and doing pretty well. He is getting excellent care. The hospital has all the medical information you gave us about Brian, so the doctors will be calling you shortly. I will get off the phone (unless you have call waiting) so you can receive that call. Here's the number of the phone I'm using to call you. You can call me, or I'll stay on as long as you would like to talk. I'll call you with every piece of news I get from the doctors."*

The family needs to know how to contact you. Remember to give them a phone number where you can be reached. Stay calm. Don't speculate about the young person's condition—positive or negative—without solid evidence to support it. Reassure the parents that their son or daughter is receiving care and that you'll keep them informed.

After contacting the parents, your next call should be to your supervisor in the youth ministry. Give him or her the essential facts about what happened and how you're handling the situation. If you are at a bank of pay phones, make this call from a different phone so the parents can reach you. (A parent will often call back immediately with additional questions after speaking with his or her spouse.) Your youth ministry supervisor can help you think through what you're doing and any logistical problems you might have. You can pray together for God's hand to be on everyone involved. Keep the line of communication open with your supervisor. Even if it's just a student with a sprain or broken bone being taken to the emergency room, you should call your supervisor. He or she can help you think through everything you should do. It's important for you and your supervisor to have discussed how you'll handle accidents in advance, so you have a clear plan when an incident occurs.

When you talk to the attending doctor, write down any information and instructions given. You should have an accurate record of what the doctor said to share with the parents. When you leave the hospital, you may have to fill a prescription for the injured student. Ask for directions to a pharmacy and make arrangements to pay for the medication.

After any accident and treatment, you should write a report describing how the injury happened, what treatment was done at the scene of the accident, and any additional treatment given by a hospital or doctor. List any witnesses to the accident and ask them to write or give you a verbal statement (you write it down, word for word) about what they saw. (A sample "Accident Report Form" is included on the CD with this book.)

If the young person stays under your supervision in the days following an injury, keep notes about his or her condition and recovery. Check on the student regularly. Stay in touch with the parents, giving them regular reports. Call them with the student and ask the parents what they want you to do and how often they want you to call. Calling too often is better than calling too little. Keep a written record of all the calls. Combine these notes with your notes on the student's condition, and submit them to your superior when you return home.

Checking back regularly with the student and the family builds good relations and shows that you care. Feeling forgotten or ignored angers parents and stimulates lawsuits.

Within a few weeks review the entire situation with your supervisor, debriefing what happened, how you responded, and what lasting impact will be felt in the ministry. Make this a learning experience to sharpen your safety procedures and first aid response. You might want to institute some new training for your workers or change how a certain event is conducted. Use the experience to make your youth ministry safer.

REFLECT AND INTERACT

Stop and reflect on your experiences and decisions related to the safety of young people. Better yet, discuss these questions with your youth ministry team:

- What first aid training do you and the members of your team have? What additional training does your youth ministry team need?

- What is the worst injury you have seen or had to respond to? How did your first aid training help you?

- Where is your first aid kit right now? Who is responsible for keeping it stocked and ready?

ARE YOU PROTECTED?

CHAPTER 16

"Young man, how many times has your outfit been sued?" The county police officer's voice was gruff as his eyes locked on mine.

"None, sir," I answered timidly.

"Well, you ought to consider yourself real lucky based on what I can see of how you operate," he replied as he returned to the paperwork for our emergency call.

The officer had responded to our call for help when a young woman complained of severe head pains and dizziness after falling and hitting her head on a rock during one of our outdoor activities in the county park. The police officer arrived minutes before the ambulance and handled our situation skillfully. But our unprofessional preparation had not won us his approval.

We'd answered almost all his questions about this young woman with responses of "I don't know" or "I'll see if someone here knows." We had no parental release form, no health history information, and no contact information for her parents. Our activity was for one afternoon—four hours with students on a school vacation day. The thought of having all that paperwork for a single four-hour event seemed like an unnecessary hassle.

Handing me a copy of his report outside the hospital emergency room, the burly officer sighed and shook his head knowingly. He didn't have to say any more. I heard him loud and clear. It was time to tighten up the way we ran our ministry events.

THREATS TO YOUR YOUTH MINISTRY

"Accidents in youth ministry aren't just probable; they're inevitable," says David Wager, director of Silver Birch Ranch in northern Wisconsin. "Despite our best efforts to prevent them, accidents will happen.

The challenge for us is to be trained and prepared to deal with them so we can save a life."

Wager believes some religious people think that if they trust in God, accidents won't happen. Consequently religious people are often poorly prepared with practical training and skills to respond to an emergency. In addition to lack of proper training, Wager lists the possibility of sexual abuse by staff, the lack of proper permission and health forms, and the substandard condition of ministry vehicles and drivers as major threats to the safety and credibility of a youth ministry.

Often safety problems reflect economic struggles. Some churches are reluctant to pay the necessary price to make the youth ministry safe. They don't think they can afford the time or money to send staff through a certified first aid program, to repair and maintain their vehicles, or to buy the insurance coverage needed to protect the young people under their care.

A small organization ran a great summer camp program for young people each year. The leaders of the camp provided much of the money for its operation out of their personal finances. When faced with the choice between spending $1800 on additional insurance coverage or purchasing new canoes and sports equipment, they opted for the canoes. A year later, after a young man died during a camp activity, the camp and its leaders were sued. They were judged to have been negligent and were ordered to pay damages far beyond the insurance coverage they carried. They lost the camp property, and several leaders had to pay large sums out of their own pockets. The ministry of that camp was halted because the leaders chose not to purchase the additional insurance.

The threat of legal action against churches and youth organizations is increasing. Litigation is growing on all fronts as people seek compensation from those they accuse of harming their children. These days, people do not hesitate to sue churches. In some states laws have been amended to remove some legal protections churches and other nonprofit organizations once had against lawsuits.

Accidents and injuries are inevitable; so are lawsuits. Youth ministries should be prepared.

NEGLIGENCE AND THE LAW

Negligence is "an unintentional breach of a legal duty causing damage reasonably foreseeable without which breach the damage would not have occurred." In lay terms it means that when young people are under your supervision, you have the responsibility to make decisions about safety and to avoid danger that any reasonable person would do. If a person is injured because a youth leader did not exhibit those safeguards, the leader is negligent and responsible.

Legally, the following tests are used to determine if negligence has occurred:

- *A Duty*—an obligation recognized by the law requiring a person to conform to a certain standard of conduct for the protection of others against unreasonable risks

- *The Act*—a failure on the part of such person to conform to the standard required

- *Proximate Cause*—a reasonably close causal connection between the conduct (failure to conform to appropriate standard) and the resulting injury

- *Damages*—actual loss or damage to the interests of another

In a lawsuit all four elements must be proven to establish a defendant is negligent and, therefore, liable to pay damages to the injured plaintiff. To establish that the defendant is not negligent, it needs to be shown that only one of the tests was not met.

The standard of care the law requires is not based on absolute safety but on reasonable actions in view of the probability of injury to others. Whether you are negligent depends upon whether you acted reasonably. This is measured by comparing your actions to what a reasonably prudent person who is charged with the stated duties would do under similar circumstances. Negligence is the failure to exercise the degree of care and sensible caution the people of a community would expect a normal person to exercise.

An additional important consideration in establishing negligence is whether an event was foreseeable. If an occurrence cannot be anticipated, a leader cannot be held responsible to provide protection against it. The question is not whether the leader wanted the incident or the subsequent consequences to happen; it's a question of whether the consequences could have been foreseen by a reasonable and prudent person. Such a person, it follows, would have taken precautions. The reason for failure to foresee the consequences—whether it is carelessness, bad judgment, excitement, simple inattention, inexperience, ignorance, stupidity, or forgetfulness—is immaterial, even though the leader was acting in good faith. The "reasonable and prudent professional" must be able to foresee when circumstances pose an "unreasonable risk of harm" against which the participant must be protected.

A detailed discussion of liability and negligence is beyond the scope of this book. These concerns should be discussed with an attorney trained in this area of law. Additional information can be obtained from books on legal liability, negligence, and risk management. For a comprehensive summary of court rulings on lawsuits related to youth activities and recreation, see the three volume set, *Legal Liability and Risk Management for Public and Private Entities*, by Betty van der Smissen (Anderson Press, 1990 with 1995 supplement).

You don't have to be a law student to have a basic understanding of negligence and the standards by which a youth leader will be judged. One purpose of this book is to help youth leaders assess their programs to determine if they are inside the boundaries of "reasonable action." The true stories contained throughout the book can help you develop a higher degree of "foreseeability" as you plan activities and events.

INSURANCE PROTECTION

A church or youth organization cannot operate without insurance. Find an insurance company and an agent that will work with you and guide you as you seek to protect the young people under your care. Three of the largest insurance companies with a special focus on insuring churches and religious groups are Brotherhood Mutual, Church Mutual, and GuideOne Insurance Companies. They offer not only insurance coverage but also training and information about how to make your youth program a safer place for kids.

WHY PARENTS SUE

1. Surprise

   The parents had no idea their kids would be doing the activity in which they were injured. Parents were not made aware of the risks their young people would be taking.

2. Lack of Communication

   Parents want information and interaction with the leaders both before any incident (as described in #1) as well as after something has happened. When the youth leaders seem unavailable or uncooperative in communicating, the parents' anger rises. Parents may also be upset if their child is injured and ministry leaders do not visit or call frequently to check on the treatment and recovery.

3. Wrong Decisions

   If parents feel leaders made a mistake in planning or allowing a certain activity, they may sue in hopes of changing the way the ministry chooses and supervises activities. Some suits are personal campaigns designed to teach people and organizations a lesson in care and safety, beyond the actual money and damages involved.

4. Covering Up

   When parents sense an organization or leader is withholding information or trying to transfer blame, they may become angry enough to sue. If parents feel an organization is more concerned about preserving its image or not suffering any financial setback more than about the condition of their injured child, they may press to assign blame.

5. Young Leaders

   When young leaders are the primary staff of an activity where an accident occurs, parents can jump to the immediate conclusion that their child was not adequately supervised. Some parents assume a young staff person is automatically inexperienced, untrained, irresponsible, and immature. Like young drivers, young leaders are often lumped together by public opinion (or insurance tables). Churches and youth organizations need clear and substantiated evidence demonstrating the training and skills of their young leaders.

What coverage should a church or youth organization consider? For the best advice, consult with a quality insurance agent. Here are my suggestions:

COMMERCIAL GENERAL LIABILITY

This type of insurance protects you in case of a lawsuit where negligence is charged. It also provides legal defense to protect the organization and any individuals named in a lawsuit. Despite strict safety practices, most organizations will be sued at some point in time. In today's North American society, it is virtually inevitable.

The amount of general liability coverage a church or organization should carry may vary according to the size of its operation, the amount of exposure (that is, the number of activities and students involved), and geographic location. Although determining a rule of thumb for the amount of coverage needed is difficult, a minimum starting figure is between $1 million and $5 million. An amount less than $1 million would not go far if, for instance, the church van had an accident in which two youth passengers were killed and six others were seriously injured. Insurance agents agree that a church can't buy too much insurance for the coverage of young people and youth activities. Emotions run high and strong when young people are injured or killed. After a tragic accident everyone wishes they had more coverage.

A reputable insurance agent can help you determine your potential liability, the level of coverage you need, and the kind of premiums you can afford. Liability insurance most often pays for the injuries and damages suffered by people we work with and care about, not strangers who are trying to get rich by suing us. Usually our coverage will be used to help the families and students who participate in our youth ministry. If they are involved in a serious injury, why should they suffer further due to our lack of planning and failure to provide adequate coverage?

A major exclusion on most general liability policies is sexual misconduct by paid or volunteer staff. The problem of sexual abuse is gaining increasing publicity as more and more young people are willing to come forward with charges against the adults who have abused them. See chapters 5 and 6 for more on issues of sexual misconduct.

ACTIVITIES MEDICAL INSURANCE

This policy focuses on accidents and sickness. It can be purchased to handle medical bills incurred by students injured in ministry activities. This coverage can handle immediate expenses and prevent families from litigating to recover medical bills.

The information and release form parents sign should indicate that any personal health insurance policy they have would be used as primary coverage in case of an injury. For families with existing coverage, the youth ministry accident policy is used as a back up for expenses their primary coverage does not handle.

Because many families today do not have medical insurance, the youth ministry or church can arrange special event insurance for a nominal fee ($1-$2 per person for each event) for a particular day or weekend or for youth ministry activities throughout the year. The easiest solution is to build the cost of the insurance into the price of the activity. The youth ministry can buy the policy for the whole group. Insurance companies offering this type of coverage want to know the number of young people covered, not a list of names stating who wants the coverage and who doesn't. When an injury occurs, the youth ministry pays the bills of families who don't have personal medical insurance. The youth ministry then submits the bills to the insurance company for reimbursement.

AUTOMOBILE LIABILITY

Coverage is needed for hired vehicles and ministry-owned autos (suggested amount—$500,000). Drivers need to be screened carefully for their motor vehicle records and should be required to carry adequate liability coverage (suggested amount: $100,000/$300,000) on their personal vehicles if they are ever allowed to drive any students. Vehicle safety and insurance is discussed in more detail in chapter 7.

WORKERS' COMPENSATION

Requirements for workers' compensation vary from state to state. Some states have lower requirements or exemptions for churches. In some states the number of employees determines an organization's

SMILE FOR THE CAMERA.

Photographs, slides, and videos can get you into trouble if you aren't careful. All the pictures taken at your events and activities are the property of the youth ministry. But if you plan to use any of the photographs, slides, videos, or audiotapes in a public setting or in a promotional piece for the youth ministry, you should have a written consent and release form from every person whose picture will be used. A sample form is included on the CD.

All pictures and recordings should be accounted for and protected from use by any unauthorized person or organization. Recently youth organizations have been warned about videotaping their activities for fear that the tapes might end up posted on the Internet or used in a courtroom as evidence in a lawsuit.

liability to provide workers' compensation. Other states have a statewide fund that handles it. Workers' compensation does apply to volunteer workers as well as paid employees—a fact that is not widely known. Staff or volunteers who are hurt while on the job (for instance, playing basketball at a retreat) might be covered for a work-related injury. Check with a local insurance agent to determine your exposure and responsibility.

ADDITIONAL INSURANCE

Coverage for watercraft, aircraft, other equipment, and activities excluded from the general liability policy can be obtained on an event-by-event basis. The premiums will be high. Liability insurance for counseling omissions and errors is recommended for professional counselors. Youth workers who counsel informally as part of their job are usually protected through the church or organization's general liability policy.

HEALTH AND LIABILITY RELEASE FORMS

Are those pieces of paper with parent signatures a worthless waste of time, or are they valuable and necessary? Most experienced youth workers have a few release-form stories to tell. Even with a signed parental release form, some hospitals still need to talk with the parents by phone before beginning treatment. Other hospitals have a contrasting procedure and attitude.

Health and liability release forms can provide valuable protection for everyone in youth ministry. In an emergency a signed health form might make the difference between a student receiving immediate care or having to wait until a family member can be contacted. Having a complete medical history gives hospital staff immediate medical information that may speed their ability to make a correct diagnosis and treatment. Having complete factual information about students, their families, and their insurance assists you in completing the extensive information forms used in most hospitals.

You can create your own forms. The sample form provided on the CD with this book can help you get started. Have an attorney and medical personnel from a local hospital review the form you decide to use. They will help you address particular information required in your local situation.

HELPFUL TIPS FOR USING MEDICAL AND RELEASE FORMS

Remember to have adult staff members complete forms, too. Their medical and family information will be needed if they're injured. Every form should be completed legibly and in ink. Printing is best. Make duplicate copies of all forms, and keep a set in your office.

A great way to get release forms from all your kids at once is to hold a parents' information meeting prior to a trip or event. Explain the activity to the parents and students. Talk about requirements and rules. Ask them to complete the forms before leaving the meeting, and have the forms notarized on the spot.

Health forms can be filled out annually (or every six months) and kept on file for students active in multiple activities that all require health forms. A parent's signature is still required for each activity to confirm that the health information given previously is current. Consult with a local lawyer about how long you should keep them in your records.

Most importantly, you must have immediate access to the forms when you need them. Make sure several people know where the forms can be found. Keep them in a central location that's easily accessed (not locked in a suitcase or the trunk of a car). While you, as the leader, should keep a full set of forms for the group, each volunteer leader on a trip should have copies of the forms for the students in his or her car or cabin.

SPECIFIC ACTIVITIES LIABILITY RELEASE FORM

While the medical information form can be stored on file and used as long as the medical information is current, the activities release form needs to be fresh and specific each time it's used. The form should describe the specific event and dates for which the parent or guardian is giving permission for the student to be involved.

Many youth workers have been told this release form is a worthless piece of paper. Its value and importance continues to be a source of debate. A signed release form does not protect a leader or group from being sued by a parent for negligence. In legal terms no organization can contract away negligence. A signed release does prove the parent or guardian gave permission for his or her child to attend the event or activity. The leader is still responsible to provide reasonable safety and protection.

One of the major causes for lawsuits involving youth programs is surprise. Parents who are not informed of the activities in which their children participate are understandably upset when something goes wrong. You can address this by providing more information to parents prior to the trip or event. You can verbally explain an activity to the parents at a pre-event meeting, but you should also put the information in writing and give it to the parents. Listing a series of risky activities and asking parents to initial their approval of their son or daughter's participation makes a much improved consent form.

Listing specific activities on the release form requires the leader to produce a fresh form for each event. Keeping the basic information in a computer file reduces the work when specific activities change.

For what events or activities is a release form needed? A lawyer will tell you to have the form completed as often as possible. The trick is to always have it when you have an accident or incident. Your standard form will cover most of your group's normal activities. I recommend always having a specific release form for the following events:

- overnight trip

- day trip out of your area

- any activity out of the ordinary

Check with a lawyer to work out the wording he or she recommends for such forms. In addition keep the lines of communication open with parents of the young people involved in your program. More contact and communication means fewer problems and reduces the chance of legal action.

Your commitment to safety and protection will be tested when a student arrives at the departure point for an overnight trip without his or her release (or medical) form. It would be very foolish to allow that person to go on the trip, despite the pressure you'll feel internally, as well as from other students. Send a message to everyone in your group about the importance of keeping the standards. Years later, they will thank you for standing strong.

Better yet, set an early deadline for the paperwork and for the money to be paid. Don't let everything wait until the last minute.

PROTECTING YOURSELF
ESTABLISH AN OVERSIGHT GROUP

Whether your ministry is large or small, ask that your church or organization establish a group of designated people to whom you will be accountable. The group could be composed of four to ten people who have interest in the youth ministry. You'll want a mixture of ages, backgrounds, and occupations. Be sure to include some parents.

Discuss your plans for the youth ministry with this oversight group. Ask for their feedback and suggestions. They are not meant to determine the strategy or goals of the ministry; they are there to give you honest feedback and help you find common-sense solutions to the problems you face. Make safety a regular item of discussion. Report to them any accidents or near misses you experience, and ask for their help as you plan future events.

If you discuss safety matters with this group and heed its advice, you will build a strong defense for the "reasonable and foreseeable" preparations you made to protect the youth attending your program. Meet at least quarterly. Keep notes of all the meetings, and file them in a safe place. On some pressurized day in the future, you'll be glad you have verification of your commitment to safety.

KEEP WRITTEN RECORDS

Most youth ministry leaders seem to hate pencils and paper. Still, leaders need to get over their fears and laziness about keeping written records. Build files and notebooks of information related to safety matters. Prepare a written report for any accident that happens in your ministry. In counseling matters keep written records of your conversations with students, noting dates and times as well as any directions or counsel you gave to a young person. Such records will be invaluable if you are ever accused of pastoral or counseling malpractice. These files should be kept under lock and key and must remain confidential. Because many lawsuits take place several years after the incident occurred, don't trust your memory to recall all the necessary facts. Written records are a must.

REMEMBER WHO YOUR PROTECTION IS

We must remember that, while we are called to cooperate and act responsibly in affairs governed by humans, we answer to a higher court and a higher judge. Everything we do and say related to safety concerns should please God and bring glory and honor to Jesus Christ.

REFLECT AND INTERACT

Stop and reflect on your experiences and decisions related to the safety of young people. Better yet, discuss these questions with your youth ministry team:

- What would make a parent sue you or your youth program?

- How does being involved in a lawsuit change people and their relationships?

- Who can help you find the appropriate insurance coverage and give you the best legal advice?

WHEN THE WORST HAPPENS

The worst day of my life was Monday, August 20, 1990. We were half-way through our YFC/Campus Life bicycle tour with 50 students plus staff riding round trip from Long Island (New York) to Maine. This day's outing was a light ride to Ogunquit, Maine (20 miles each way), for a fun day at the ocean.

We never made it to the beach. As the adult leader I was riding in the next-to-last spot in the single-file line of eight bikers. My experienced college-age leader was in front, leading the way. I was doing my job, reminding the riders about being careful and warning them about the traffic approaching from behind.

Suddenly, Kim Masterson, one of the young women riding in the middle of our line, lost her balance and began to fall to her left into the road. The more she fought to regain her balance, the deeper her bike veered into the traffic. Everything seemed to go into slow motion as we watched a vehicle collide with Kim. That picture is still clear in my mind though nearly two decades have passed.

I jumped from my bike and rushed to Kim, who was lying on the road. Checking her vital signs, I could not detect any indication of life. A doctor at the hospital would later confirm she had died instantly from massive multiple traumas. In the midst of indescribable chaos, I quickly checked to see if anyone else in the group had been injured and organized them to call an ambulance, stop the traffic, and begin helping me.

I quickly prayed for Kim and asked God to give me the strength and wisdom I needed for that moment. I began rescue breathing and CPR while trying to control the bleeding and other apparent injuries in an attempt to restore Kim's vital signs and give her every possible chance. The ambulance crew arrived within 15 minutes and took over the treatment.

WHAT SUDDEN DEATH DOES TO SURVIVORS

- Leaves them with a sense of unreality about the loss.
- Provokes feelings of intense guilt and incredible rage.
- Raises a strong need to blame someone.
- Causes a sense of helplessness.
- Leaves a lingering sense of unfinished business.
- Creates an intense need to understand why the death happened.
- Brings scrutiny from legal and medical authorities and the media.

J. Worden
Grief Counseling and Grief Therapy: A Handbook for the Mental Health Practitioner

While I was attending to Kim, the junior leader had found a motorist with a car phone to call the emergency number. The traffic had stopped in both directions. I remember seeing women leave their cars to come to the aid of the students in our group. The students who had not been assigned a job were shaking and crying. These women embraced the young people and comforted them as the emergency procedures continued. One of our guys ran back up the road to stop the next approaching bike group. I'd told him to keep them at least 200 feet away from the scene.

When Kim was placed in the ambulance, a police detective asked me to ride with him to the hospital. I quickly ran back to the other leaders of the bike group who were sitting in hushed silence 200 feet away and instructed them to work out all the necessary logistics. The police were outstanding in helping us respond to all the problems this accident presented. On the way to the hospital, I spotted our support van sitting in the stalled traffic. When I stepped out of the police car, their worst fears were confirmed. From the files in the van, I pulled all the information we had on Kim to take with me to the hospital. The staff in the van were given clearance to move ahead and work with the police to help the remaining bikers.

My head was spinning. My heart was breaking. I stiffened every part of my insides to try to maintain control of myself. At the hospital the confirmation of Kim's death came quickly. In my 19 years of working with youth up to that point, I'd always prayed I'd never be in a hospital room and hear those words. The impact of what Kim's death would mean for her family and everyone else involved began to hit me hard.

I was driven to the police station where we started the paperwork and the process of contacting Kim's parents back on Long Island. I called their pastor with the news. He traveled with the Long Island police (who'd been contacted by the Maine police) to the parents' place of business. They delivered the bad news to Kim's mom and dad and then called me at the Maine police station. On previous trips I'd often chided kids about safety, telling them I wouldn't know what to say if I ever had to call their parents. The experience was every bit as difficult as I'd expected. The police sergeant stood beside me and coached me through the call. Even in the midst of their own shock and grief, Kim's parents were so thoughtful in expressing their concern for me and everyone else on the trip.

My next calls were to the Long Island YFC office, our local board chairman, and my wife. They started the process of informing the national YFC office and the parents of all students on the trip. While I was calling Long Island, the police sergeant was contacting a local youth agency to request help for our group.

This was a key moment in the whole process. I would never have thought to request such help, especially from a secular agency. I needed plenty of help, but the emotional tidal wave sweeping over me hindered my ability to function rationally and determine what needed to be done. I was already experiencing a "walking shock" and was in no position to do any more than I'd already been trained to do. After taking me through his part of the process, the police sergeant had the compassion and foresight to pass me on to people who could help me face the problems still ahead.

RESPONSE TO SUDDEN DEATH

No one wants to think about it, but it's very possible you will be faced with a sudden death situation—either in your group or with someone connected to your students. Most high schools lose at least one student each school year to a car accident or some personal tragedy. While no one is ever fully prepared for such a situation, I hope my experience will encourage you to think carefully about how you and your ministry team might respond in such circumstances.

I will always be grateful for the team of counselors from a variety of agencies that came together to provide emergency care for us. The actions of this response team provides a model for helping youth groups who have experienced a sudden death or a severe injury while on a trip away from home.

Within an hour of making the phone calls to Kim's parents, I was in a local hospital meeting with a team of six mental healthcare workers and counselors. They were prepared to help me develop a plan to take the news of Kim's death back to our group. All the students and staff had returned by bus to the youth home where we'd stayed the previous night. The counseling team helped me plan the logistics of canceling the rest of the trip and returning home. They spent the first hour of the meeting helping me understand the special counseling needs our students would require during the 24 hours before we traveled home. The coordinator of the team showed great sensitivity toward our Christian faith. One of the people selected for the team was from a local Christian counseling center. The fact that he'd served as a YFC director some years prior helped the other workers understand our group. All of them showed generous love and care for me and the burdens I carried during those hours.

The police called ahead before returning me to the youth home where all the students and staff were waiting for some word about Kim. They arranged for me to meet immediately with half of the staff and some of Kim's closest friends. After meeting with them, we met with the rest of the staff and finally gathered the whole group to break the news. The team of counselors accompanied me and coached me as I delivered the bad news in each session. They spread themselves among the staff and young people and helped them talk about their feelings.

For 19 hours (from four that afternoon until eleven the next morning when we boarded the chartered bus) the local team of counselors was on site with us, available to talk and comfort anyone who needed help. The team broke our group into significant subgroups according to the impact of the accident on each person. They assigned counselors to each group and responded according to the needs they observed.

Our biking group (seven of us) met in a private room with the team coordinator to discuss what had happened. This group was the most deeply traumatized because we'd seen the accident and the emergency efforts. The counselor asked us to agree that we'd talk about what we'd seen only within our group. Others on the trip did not need to know the details of the tragedy we'd witnessed. We were then asked to share in full detail what we'd seen that morning. Everyone had great difficulty speaking aloud. Earlier a woman at the police department had given me six

> ## HOW TO SURVIVE A TRAUMATIC EXPERIENCE
> - Don't be afraid to cry.
> - Find someone who is a good listener.
> - Take time to heal.
> - Expect setbacks.
> - Don't make any major decisions.
> - Get involved in a support group.
>
> Iris Bolton, *Know You Can Survive*

large teddy bears to give to any of Kim's special friends. At the time I thought the gift was totally inappropriate, but at the counselor's suggestion I distributed them in our group. Having something soft to hold and squeeze seemed to help some people get out the words and the tears.

When I shared with the group, my whole body shook uncontrollably as I described what I had witnessed and had done at the scene of the accident. Later that night when I struggled to stay awake (I was afraid of having a nightmare), I wandered into the dining room and spoke with a counselor. Half of our group stayed up most of the night talking, playing board games, and spending time with the counselors. As much as I hated it, talking about the details did bring some relief.

The next morning we had a large group meeting with some singing and testimonies about Kim and her strong Christian faith. We concluded with a short talk about what the Bible says about death and what happened to Kim when she died.

The counseling team stayed with us until we were loaded on the bus. They gave instruction to us about what we would experience in the days ahead. They helped us realize our intense feelings were quite normal. We felt as though we were leaving special friends when we said good-bye.

The bus ride home took seven hours. Although our emotions had been drained during the 24 hours in Maine, the parents and friends who greeted us were bursting with emotion. Every family situation was highly charged with a variety of feelings. No one could escape what had happened to us. The next three days, which included the wake (viewing/visitation) and Kim's funeral, were an emotional roller coaster. We were drawing on our Christian faith for all it could provide. We were experiencing feelings and thoughts entirely different than any we'd ever known. Kim's parents greeted us lovingly and showed great concern for our needs. Their support and kindness buoyed our YFC staff.

The night after the funeral, we held an open house for any student or parent who wanted to attend. Counselors from a local hospital who specialized in assisting victims of trauma volunteered their services. The next few Friday nights, we gathered many students from the trip together for times of games, music, snacks, and talk.

After Kim's funeral the group most resistant to counseling was the staff. We had several sessions where counselors found it very difficult to get staff members to share their feelings. We stopped after only two sessions at the staff's request. I personally went to a counselor weekly for four months and felt the benefit of opening up with him.

For all my experience in planning bike trips, I'd never considered a contingency plan for a death or serious injury. I would never have considered how a team of local counselors could assist our group. But the team that came together to support us in the hours after Kim's death helped us release our thoughts and emotions with their quiet, listening style. These professionals supported our staff and taught us how to respond to a sudden death. In less than 24 hours, they gave us a foundation from which we could step off into the grieving process. The team of trauma counselors who met with us when we returned home helped us handle our feelings about the funeral and the tensions we felt as we reentered our families. Each group played a special role at a crucial time. Some staff and students took advantage of their services; others did not. It was important to have these services available.

HOW THE COUNSELING TEAMS HELPED OUR GROUP

THEY HELPED THE LEADER BY:

- providing practical help and emotional support.
- coordinating logistics (arranged food, buses, phone calls).
- formulating a 24-hour plan.
- providing personal counseling.

THEY PREPARED A COUNSELING STRATEGY BY:

- dividing people into groups according to the level of trauma.
- taking leadership with each group.
- devising a strategy to break the news sensitively.
- responding to special people and their needs.

THEY EDUCATED THE STAFF BY:

- helping us deal with our own grief.
- telling us how to help others handle their grief.
- telling us what to expect in the days and weeks ahead.

PREPARING FOR TRAUMATIC SITUATIONS

Obviously no one knows when a tragedy will strike his or her group.

The leader is responsible for providing emergency preparedness for the youth ministry staff and the youth of the church. Normally we would not seek help until we need it, but it is wise to be prepared for the worst. Emergency preparedness does not apply only to accidental deaths but also to suicides and disabling injuries that might occur in the group.

WHO CAN HELP US RESPOND?

It's important to think about who could help you respond in the event of a tragedy. Which hospital in your area has a trauma team? Familiarize yourself with its services. Keep the phone number and contact names in your personal records and in the church records.

The key person to find is a competent trauma team coordinator. This person should be aware of the resources in the community and how to access them. A youth group leader cannot put together all the pieces of logistics, counseling, and response when he or she is part of the tragedy. Plan ahead by identifying several people in your community who could fill that role.

Other sources of help include:

- Hotlines. Keep a list of contacts and specific services offered.

- Police, fire, and emergency squads. They not only offer immediate assistance, but also know of additional community resources.

- Support organizations such as Compassionate Friends and other survivor groups. Check their listings in the phone book.

- Prayer chains. What churches in your area have active prayer chains that can quickly mobilize people to pray for a traumatic situation? Keep their phone numbers readily available.

- Therapists and counselors. Who in your community is trained and willing to help in an emergency?

- Ministers. Who in your community is trained or experienced in counseling people through grief and trauma? Make a list.

- Healthcare professionals on church or organization boards. These people are close to ministry and have professional skills to offer.

- Bereavement groups. These groups can help students and staff find long-term support.

PREPARE TO EDUCATE STUDENTS AND STAFF

Given the probability that some kind of traumatic event will affect your youth group or a student in your group, you should prepare an information sheet on what people should expect to experience. On the CD included with this book, you'll find a sample sheet that lists some of the emotional, mental, physical, and behavioral reactions people often experience in the wake of a traumatic event. This written information can be given to them at the appropriate time along with verbal counseling you provide.

DEALING WITH EMOTIONAL AFTERSHOCKS

Every trauma will bring emotional aftershocks. Here are some suggestions for coping with them:

- Within the first 24 to 48 hours, perform some strenuous physical exercise alternated with relaxation.

- Structure your time and keep busy.

- Realize you are normal and your reactions are normal.

- Talk to people. Talking is the most healing medicine.

COMMON PROGRESSION OF FEELINGS WHEN REACTING TO A DEATH OR DISABLING INJURY

- High Anxiety/Emotional Shock—not in touch with feelings.
- Denial—"This can't be happening."
- Anger—strong emotional reactions of all types from screaming to depression; person is less capable of handling any extra pressure.
- Remorse (Bargaining)—"If only I had done this . . . "
- Grief—dealing with the loss, saying goodbye, and preparing to move on.
- Reconciliation (Acceptance)—ready to move on; "Okay, this happened; I'll find a way to deal with it and move ahead with my life."

- Don't try to numb your pain with drugs or alcohol.

- Reach out to the people trying to help you.

- Maintain a normal schedule.

- Spend time with others.

- Keep a journal, and write your way through the sleepless hours.

- Don't make any big decisions.

- Get plenty of rest.

- Accept recurring thoughts, dreams, and flashbacks as normal. Don't fight them. They will decrease over time and become less painful.

- Eat well-balanced and regular meals (even when you don't feel like it).

- Share your feelings and thoughts with others.

To help a friend or family member deal with emotional aftershocks:

- Listen carefully.

- Be available to spend time with the person, but also allow space for private time.

- Offer assistance and a listening ear.

- Reassure the person that he or she is safe.

- Help with everyday tasks.

- Don't take the affected person's anger or other feelings personally.

- Don't tell the person he or she is "lucky it wasn't worse." Such statements do not console traumatized people.

- Tell the person you are sorry the event happened and you want to understand and assist him or her.

- Remind the person that confusing emotions are normal.

- Don't attempt to impose your explanation on why the event happened.

- Don't tell the person you know how it feels. You probably don't.

- Be willing to say nothing. Just being there is often the best support you can give.

- Offer to accompany the person to any meetings or appointments that concern the event.

- Don't ask for details of the trauma. If the person wants to talk, just listen. Let him or her know you are there and care. It isn't necessary to try to make things better. Offer to pray with them and for them.

- Read passages of assurance and hope from the Bible.

DEALING WITH A SUICIDE IN OR NEAR YOUR GROUP

Like the survivors of other tragic events, the friends and family of a person who commits suicide experience a profound bereavement process filled with questions. They are often overwhelmed by the intensity of their feelings. They

NOTHING TO HIDE

After a fatal accident or serious injury, the leader must immediately file a written report detailing everything that happened before, during, and after the incident. Be sure to list other witnesses, and obtain statements from them. This should be done within seven days of the incident, while the events are still clear in people's minds. File these reports with your governing board or supervisor for safekeeping. The police will be asking for statements from the leader and all witnesses. Warn the young people involved and their families to be very careful about speaking to the media. Usually it is best to refuse comment.

If you become the subject of a lawsuit, secure legal counsel. Your church or organization can help you respond appropriately. If you are properly insured, the insurance carrier will cover your legal defense. Do not make any statements about the matter to the public or the media. Conduct yourself with honesty and integrity, remembering the pain and suffering the person bringing the lawsuit is experiencing.

often feel very angry with the person for ending his or her life. They feel guilt and remorse over what might have been done to help the person. They recognize calls for help that they overlooked prior to the suicide. The survivors often feel hopeless and depressed.

Supporting the survivors starts by encouraging them to express their feelings. Provide places to talk and comfortable ways to bring up the subject. Teach survivors about the grief process so they can understand their feelings are normal. Help them call upon their faith in God. Stress God's plan and purpose for them. Encourage them to participate in a weekly support group for several months or more. If necessary arrange for them to seek professional help.

DEALING WITH A DISABLING INJURY

Some people believe a disabling injury is even more stressful than a death because of its long-term impact on the lives of everyone involved. The shock of such an injury is similar to what people feel when someone is killed. The last step of the grieving process is reconciling to the new situation and deciding to move ahead. The disabled person and his or her family and friends must go through a similar process to reach that conclusion.

There are many helpful books and training classes available to assist people in reacting to such injuries and adjusting to live productive lives. Support groups for friends and family members provide a place to vent their feelings and frustrations among people who have had similar experiences.

RETURNING TO "NORMAL"

After your youth group experiences a death or a disabling injury, returning to ministry the way it was before the event is virtually impossible. Spiritually, the best place to start is where the group finds itself. Lessons can be refocused to give attention to issues raised by the accident. The format of the ministry should include plenty of opportunities for open and honest sharing. When awkward moments come just acknowledge how everyone is feeling and move ahead with a positive statement about the person and what the group has been through. The goal is to help everyone accept the fact of the accident and move forward. The leader's good example can set the tone for the group. If the leader acknowledges his or her own need for help, seeks counseling, and talks openly about what happened, it helps the attitude of the whole group.

You may wonder if your group can ever return to the same activity or location of the accident. We were encouraged by Kim's parents to continue our bike trips. Their vocal support made it a much easier decision. We reexamined our safety procedures and committed ourselves to continue our high standards of safety. Since the accident we have conducted other long trips without incident. About half of the students who were on the trip when the accident occurred rode with us again over the next two years. We tried to create an atmosphere where we could talk about our fears and feelings openly. It was a real life lesson in overcoming fear.

I hope you'll never experience the death of a young person during one of your youth ministry activities. I hope my story and the rest of this book have motivated you to commit your best efforts to protecting the health and safety of your students. But tragic events still happen sometimes, in spite of our best efforts to prevent them. If one of your students is ever killed or disabled, I hope this account provides an outline that will help you deal with the tragedy. You can be confident that God will provide the strength you need in those trying moments.

REFLECT AND INTERACT

Stop and reflect on your experiences and decisions related to the safety of young people. Better yet, discuss these questions with your youth ministry team:

- What experiences have you had with a serious accident or accidental death in youth ministry?
- How did those experiences change you?
- What can we do better to help prepare our students to deal with the sudden death of one of their peers?

DEAR LORD, GUARD AND PROTECT US

How safety conscious was Jesus? Imagine his reaction if one of his disciples had spoken up when he invited Peter to step out of the boat and onto the water? "Excuse me, Jesus, but shouldn't Peter be wearing a personal flotation device approved by the Roman Legion Coast Guard?"

Does being strong on safety practices contradict the life of faith we seek to live? If we are strong in prayer, believe the Bible, and are led by the Spirit, should safety procedures and practices be a big concern to us?

For many youth workers the subjects of safety and spirituality pose no contradictions. It's not either/or; it's both/and. But for those in youth work who hold on to faith and prayer as the only line of safety—and for others who hide lazy safety habits behind a theological screen—I present these six frequently asked questions (and answers).

DOES LIVING BY FAITH MEAN TAKING SAFETY RISKS?

Praying in faith and practicing common sense are not contradictory. A mature Christian seeks to develop a growing, integrated package of common sense, spirituality, and wisdom. Even though we build our youth ministry on God's Word and prayer, we don't need a Bible passage or prayer session to tell us we should wear a life jacket in deep, fast water. God is good. He gave us a brain to handle some of the obvious choices of daily life.

If a secular person and a spiritual person are both standing on the bank of the river deciding if their respective youth groups should go into the water, they should reach the same conclusion. The spiritual person isn't demonstrating any lack of faith by deciding not to canoe the river. In fact the spiritual person has even better reasons for his or her decision. The spiritual person knows the lives under his or her responsibility are special, unique creations of God. This youth leader recognizes the fallen world as a dangerous place with pain, suffering, and death caused by a universal rebellion against God. He or she lives to glorify God and to reflect the character of God to everyone he or she contacts. This person realizes handling young lives carelessly does not reflect the character of God.

CAN'T GOD PROTECT US? WHY SHOULD WE TRY TO PROTECT OURSELVES?

Some people argue that the Christian life is built on putting our trust in God alone, not by following the conventions of human beings. Therefore, they say, the Christian youth program operating by faith can take risks, because God will guide and protect.

Don't believe it. God is capable of rescuing people from any hazardous situation, but that doesn't mean we should test him or defy the forces of nature. In the desert Satan challenged Jesus to throw himself off the top of the Temple because God would provide angels to catch him. Jesus replied, "It is said, 'Do not put the Lord your God to the test'" (Luke 4:12). Conducting youth ministry without a safety plan and depending on God alone to protect us is putting God to the test. That's not faith; it's foolishness.

Will God protect us when we don't plan for safety or use common sense? He may—but that's the wrong question. The real question is, "Are we wise or are we foolish?" Proverbs 28:26 says, "Those who trust in themselves are fools, but those who walk in wisdom are kept safe." So what does it mean to walk in wisdom?

To trust and honor God.

To know what God has said in his written Word.

To make right choices.

To learn from our mistakes.

The spiritual, safety-conscious youth leader walks in wisdom. We learn through prayer but also through life experiences that teach us common sense. When we reflect God's character and values, safety becomes a strong motivation. We plan for safety because every young life is valued and treasured by God. If God cares for the kids under our care, shouldn't we use every ounce of our ability to do the same? How can young people believe God loves them if the youth ministry leaders who tell them of God's love put them in dangerous situations with little regard for their safety?

The wise youth worker prays diligently about the safety of his or her students, calling on God to point out what needs to be done to protect each young person. This leader learns from his or her own mistakes and by listening to others. He or she sets aside pride and ego to gain a teachable attitude. This book provides youth workers with true-life lessons they can apply to the safety choices they will make. Being wise means learning those lessons and applying them to the way we live.

CAN'T WE JUST PRAY AND GO FOR IT?

I was speaking at a youth workers' training session during the early stages of writing this book. I shared the story of Larry, the youth director who had to decide if he'd take his group canoeing in a swollen river (see chapter 1). Before revealing Larry's decision I asked the 85 youth leaders what they would do.

One lively, strapping guy said, "I'd get those kids out of the van. We'd have some serious prayer time and then go for it." The other leaders exploded with response. Half of them seemed energized by his spiritual enthusiasm and confidence that God hears prayers and watches over his children when they step out in faith. The other half seemed shocked at the suggestion of exposing young people to such an obvious life-threatening risk.

The questions bounced off the walls. What kind of serious prayer session does it take to get inexperienced canoeists safely down a swollen river? How do you know if your prayer has been serious enough? Does serious prayer mean talking loud and long to God or listening quietly and carefully to God? One leader in the training session asked, "If this were really a serious prayer session, wouldn't God tell someone in that circle that it wasn't safe for them to be in the river?"

We misunderstand prayer when we treat it like a magic insurance policy. We can't do whatever we want and expect God to protect us just because we got two or three to agree in Jesus' name. This is a fundamental issue of prayer. Do we pray to tell God what we want him to do for us or are we supposed to be listening for some indication of what he wants us to do for him?

I believe a youth leader's prayer should sound something, such as, this: "Lord, as we lead this youth ministry, point out to us what is ungodly, unproductive, and unsafe. Show us how to change it, so we will take care of these young people the way you would and be a better witness for your name."

HOW CAN SAFETY BE A WITNESS FOR JESUS?

As I interviewed youth leaders for this book, there was a "part two" to nearly every story of an accident or tragedy they told. It concerned the faith of the student and his or her family in the months and years after the incident. Many youth workers told of students and parents who were turned off to the church and the Christian faith because they felt the youth ministry had put them (or their child) in jeopardy.

The students who were betrayed and sexually abused had the most severe reaction to their leaders. Many of them sunk into deep rebellion against God and doubted the sincerity of any Christian leader. Their friends, shocked and angry with the abusing adult leader, often joined them in falling away from the faith. Those who were hurt physically during ministry activities tended to be more forgiving. But in situations where the parents felt youth leaders were careless or nonchalant about safety, walls went up between the youth ministry and the whole family.

Every youth ministry staff person needs to hear Jesus' warning with fresh ears: "If anyone causes one of these little ones—those who believe in me—to stumble, it would be better for them if a large millstone were hung around their neck and they were drowned in the depths of the sea" (Matthew 18:6). God will drop the hammer on those who seduce and sexually or physically abuse kids. This warning extends to youth leaders who cause the hearts of young people and parents to harden toward God because of youth ministries that lacked care and responsibility.

Safety is a positive witness to young people and their parents. If you seek to be a witness for Christ to an unchurched family, one of the very best ways to create interest and involvement is to demonstrate how much you care for their children. In nearly 40 years as a youth ministry leader, I've seen countless parents positively impacted for Christ because of the dedicated concern and care our adult leaders showed for their teenagers. The skill and professionalism we demonstrated through the organization of our activities and the care provided when a young person was ill or injured won the admiration and interest of the parents.

All the young people in our groups are precious resources entrusted to us by God (and their parents) for care and handling. How we treat them shapes their lives. We cannot accept any policy that treats kids less safely than their parents would. Living up to God's treatment standards is even more challenging.

CAN'T ACCIDENTS BE GOD'S WILL?

Another leader at the training session asked, "Whatever happened to the sovereignty of God? We can't be worrying about everything that might happen to our kids. What's wrong with just trusting that whatever happens is the will of God? Aren't we trying to do God's job by being so paranoid about safety?"

When Kim Masterson was killed on our bicycle trip, I asked a thousand "what if" and "why" questions. The original plan for the trip had us riding that stretch of road a day earlier, but it poured heavy rain that day. Since we had an extra day on our schedule, we decided not to put ourselves on the road in those conditions. The day of the accident was bright and sunny. If we had ridden the previous day in the rain, would we have avoided the accident and Kim's death? Kim was a last-minute registrant on the trip, headed for her freshman year of college as soon as she returned home. If she'd been home preparing for college on that day, would she have died in different circumstances? Had God appointed that day as her last day on earth? Was it God's will for Kim to die that day on a road in Maine? I don't think I'll ever know the answers to those questions while I am on this earth.

I do have great confidence in the sovereignty of God. I believe that God works out all things for our good (Romans 8:28). That promise doesn't mean, however, that every occurrence, everything that happens to us, is good. The evil in our fallen world produces an environment that includes pain, suffering, and death. What is remarkable is God's ability to use even these terrible events for our long-term good. In our hedonistic world I need a constant reminder that God is not working to make me happy but to fulfill his purpose.

Yet my confidence in the sovereignty of God is no reason to relax my best human efforts to keep everyone on a youth ministry trip safe from danger. Life is precious, and my job (both inside and outside of youth ministry) is to protect it.

I would challenge those who argue that God's sovereignty is a reason we need not give our best effort for safety. Do you leave your house unlocked because you believe that, if God's will is for your house to be robbed, it will happen regardless of what precautions you might take? Most people don't. They trust God to provide protection, but they do their part by locking their doors. Godly common sense recognizes the dangers of this world and responds appropriately. If we take steps to protect our money and our valuables, can we say we love young people if we don't take the best precautions to protect those God has placed in our care?

We live in a fallen, sinful world governed by physical laws and natural forces. We plan our steps according to those forces. Although God is both capable and caring, we shouldn't plan our youth ministry expecting that God will suspend the laws of physics when we shoot up a 911 prayer. Even strong Christians don't hold a prayer service in the middle of a lake, holding up a large metal cross during a thunderstorm.

WHEN ACCIDENTS HAPPEN, HAS GOD FAILED US?

A friend told me I shouldn't pray for safety in front of the students in our group. She was concerned that students might lose faith in God's ability to answer our prayers if we ever have a serious accident and someone is hurt or killed.

If an accident happens, does it mean God didn't hear our prayers for safety? Perhaps we're shielded from seeing how God protected us from a greater disaster. Maybe we should thank God that nothing worse happened to our group. Perhaps we are guilty of taking for granted all the instances of God's protection we don't see each day. We need to keep praying with intensity for God's hand to be on all we do.

After an accident some students and staff may feel strongly that God doesn't care. When Job struggled through his calamities, he learned that we humans cannot always understand the reasons why something occurred. Sometimes the answers and explanations are held back. Believing in God or prayer does not protect us from trouble. Rather, it prepares us to handle what life in a fallen world brings to us. The message of Job is not to give up. God may allow suffering in our lives for reasons we can't understand. But our faith and trust in God can grow through that process.

Jay Kesler, former president of Taylor University, has said we have three choices when there is a tragic accident: One, we can believe there is no God; two, we can believe God causes these things to happen; or three, we can understand that God allows these things to happen without causing them. God has created a physical universe with natural laws that govern how we live. Sometimes gravity saves a person's life; other times gravity pulls a person to his or her death. Everything we know about God tells us that when accidents happen, God shares the sorrow of the people who are involved.

FINAL THOUGHTS

Is it heresy to say that the health and safety of the young people in our care is the number one responsibility of Christian youth workers? If we say that, does it mean we think sharing the love of God and the need for a personal relationship with Jesus is a lower priority? On the contrary, I think caring for the health and safety of our young people is an essential part of communicating God's love for them.

For people to believe the message of God's love, they must trust the messenger. God has placed youth ministers in a strategic position to change the lives of entire families. This mission begins with trust. If parents and students know the youth ministry staff cares so much for them that their top priority is to protect their safety, they will be open to the message they bring. Lack of planning and care for safety is not only criminal, it is a terrible witness for Christ.

Attention to safety concerns brings glory to the name of Christ. It shows love and concern. It lays the foundation for future trust when the life-changing message of Jesus is presented. Safety concerns are not a contradiction to a life of faith. In youth ministry safety concerns open the door for people to discover a life of faith.

REFLECT AND INTERACT

Stop and reflect on your experiences and decisions related to the safety of young people. Better yet, discuss these questions with your youth ministry team:

- How do your Christian beliefs shape your attitude and actions about safety?

- Does a Christian youth leader feel more or less safe than an atheistic youth leader?

- In what tangible ways do students and parents see evidence of your love and concern for their well being?

- How do you explain why an accident happened when you and others prayed for safety and God's protection?

DIRECTORY OF SAMPLE FORMS AND INFORMATION ON THE BETTER SAFE THAN SUED CD

EVALUATION TOOLS:

HOW SAFE IS YOUR YOUTH MINISTRY?

SAMPLE FORMS AND POLICIES:

SAMPLE MINISTRY VEHICLE POLICY STATEMENT

SAMPLE FORM FOR DESIGNATED DRIVERS

SAMPLE ACCIDENT/INJURY REPORT FORM

SAMPLE HEALTH INFORMATION FORM

SAMPLE PARENT INFORMATION AND RELEASE FORM

SAMPLE STUDENT INFORMATION AND CODE OF BEHAVIOR AGREEMENT

SAMPLE PERMISSION FORM FOR USE OF PHOTOGRAPHS AND OTHER VIDEO/AUDIO MATERIAL

SAFETY INFORMATION HANDOUTS:

12 BASIC PRINCIPLES OF SAFETY FOR YOUTH MINISTRY

THE COMMON SAFETY SINS OF YOUTH MINISTRY

STAFF/STUDENT APPROPRIATE CONDUCT STANDARDS

SAFETY TIPS FOR SWIMMING

CANOEING SAFETY CHECKLIST

BOATING SAFETY PRINCIPLES

WATERSKIING SAFETY PRINCIPLES

SKIING AND SNOWBOARDING SAFETY GUIDELINES

BEFORE YOU HIKE: LEADER PREPARATION

BASIC STEPS OF FIRST AID

TRAUMATIC EVENT STRESS INFORMATION SHEET

Don't let burnout force you out! Exhaustion, frustration, disappointment, and conflict bring many youth workers to a point where they either choose a new church, a new career, or someone makes that choice for them. Inside this book you'll find steps you can take to help build fences against failure, and you'll learn what it takes to survive and thrive in youth ministry.

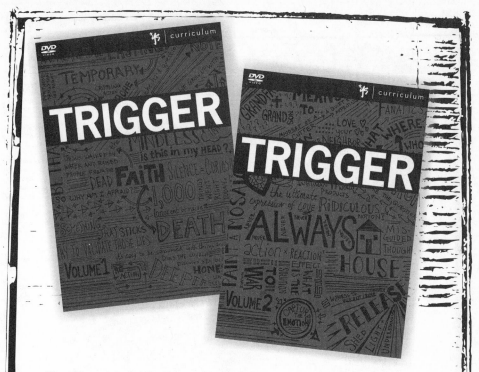

The Trigger series is the perfect addition to your large group, small group, or Sunday school program. The video vignettes will open your students' eyes and hearts to issues that really matter, and will open conversations that can change lives.

On Volume 1 you'll see videos about faith, death, innocence, relationships, everyday life, and motives. And on Volume 2 you'll see videos about evangelism, the Church, cutting, war and violence, and loving others. Both volumes contain pdf discussion guides to help you lead engaging conversations.

Trigger Volume 1
Passenger Productions
RETAIL $24.99
ISBN 978-0-310-28072-9

Trigger Volume 2
Passenger Productions
RETAIL $24.99
ISBN 978-0-310-28073-6

In this new DVD series from the Skit Guys, you'll find everything you need to teach a memorable lesson to your students on topics that really matter to them. Tommy & Eddie provide you with a Skit Guys video, a message outline, and small group questions for each lesson—making it easier than ever for you to plan a lesson!

You Teach Vol. 1
Videos, Study Guides, and Sermon Illustrations
The Skit Guys: Eddie James and Tommy Woodard
RETAIL $39.99
ISBN 978-0-310-28084-2

You Teach Vol. 2
Videos, Study Guides, and Sermon Illustrations
The Skit Guys: Eddie James and Tommy Woodard
RETAIL $39.99
ISBN 978-0-310-28085-9